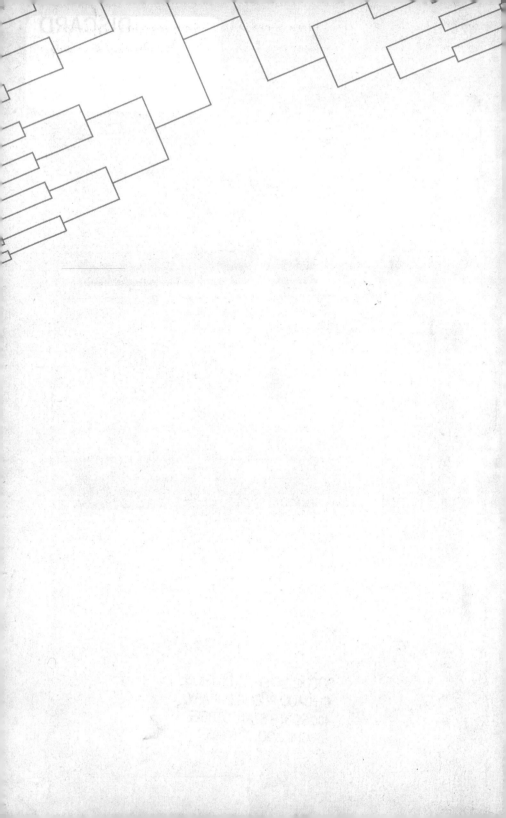

The
Madness
of March

Bonding and Betting with the Boys in Las Vegas

Alan Jay Zaremba

University of Nebraska Press | Lincoln and London

∞

Library of Congress Cataloging-in-Publication Data

Zaremba, Alan Jay.
The madness of March : bonding and betting with
the boys in Las Vegas / Alan Jay Zaremba.
p. cm.
ISBN 978-0-8032-1383-8 (pbk. : alk. paper)
1. Basketball—Betting—Nevada—Las Vegas.
2. College sports—Corrupt practices—Nevada—
Las Vegas. I. Title.
GV887.7.Z37 2009
796.323'630973—dc22
2008034067

Set in Janson by Bob Reitz.
Designed by Joel Gehringer.

According to family lore, when I was
five months old my father was holding
me while watching a closely contested
basketball game. At a particularly
thrilling juncture Dad became so excited
that he bolted up from his chair and
tossed me unintentionally into the air.

Apparently I come honestly by my
enthusiasm for sports and interest in
those who are similarly enthusiastic. It
is appropriate then that I dedicate this
book about college basketball and its
fans to my father, Meyer Zaremba, who
may have tossed me in the air that day,
but on that day and all others never
failed to be there with his arms open
wide to catch me on the way down.

Contents

Prologue

Dan Rather

The first weekend of the NCAA basketball tournament brings a dedicated legion of basketball bettors to Las Vegas. From early Thursday morning until Sunday evening, men—and the crowd is overwhelmingly male—sit in rowdy smoky casinos watching up to forty-eight college basketball games. Who are these people? They pay to fly out to Las Vegas, spend money on lodging, sit for four days straight watching basketball games, and often lose hundreds of dollars on near misses and if onlys, and yet as they taxi to the airport on Sunday evening they are planning their betting strategy for the following year with undiminished passion.

In March 2003 the NCAA considered canceling the NCAA tournament because the start of the games coincided with the beginning of the Iraq war. On Tuesday evening, March 18, during an internationally televised address, President George Bush announced that Saddam Hussein had twenty-four hours to give himself up. If Hussein did not do so, sometime after the twenty-four hours had elapsed the United States would strike.

On Wednesday night—twenty-four hours later to the minute—two planeloads of basketball bettors waited by an America West gate at New York's Kennedy airport for their flights to Las Vegas. Both flights were completely sold out. Above the bar where the travelers were clustered, television anchors described the beginnings of the war.

The men at the bar paid no attention to newscaster Peter Jennings. They were looking at their NCAA tournament brackets.

On Thursday morning, hours after the United States had launched its attack, the tension at the Tampa International airport was palpable. Reporters randomly asked passengers if they were unnerved. Baggage underwent more scrutiny than usual, and security at the airport was extensive. I boarded my Southwest flight to Las Vegas with some anxiety. I was not settled into my seat for more than two minutes when a fellow in front of me—a stranger—turned around and asked me if I thought Marquette could cover the spread.

Later that day I was seated in the Paris Hotel on Las Vegas Boulevard—the Strip—watching the games. The Paris theater was filled with bettors from all over the country who, apparently, were not troubled by the international crisis. Four movie screens were suspended from the ceiling above the stage. The well-oiled spectators who filled the theater were focused on the four basketball games projected on the giant screens. When Dan Rather periodically interrupted the contests with reports from Baghdad, the booing in the theater was deafening.

Who Are These Guys

The first words he reads in the morning are in the sports section of the newspaper. He pores over these pages while drinking coffee, chewing his toast, and using the bathroom. He studies box scores like a scholar examining minute details of important texts.

At the end of the week, when he picks up the clutter that has accrued in the apartment, he finds folded-up sports pages from days ago that have been left near the toilet.

He is familiar with the traditional fall, winter, spring, and summer seasonal designations but nevertheless tends to identify portions of the year by what sport is played. Autumn is not so much autumn as it is football season. April does not mark the beginning of spring, but baseball season. His index to personal history uses this method to organize and recollect data. "Sure, I remember when I had my last checkup. It was during football season. It was on a Monday after the game when the Packers beat the Bears in overtime."

He can identify the entire rosters of the teams to which he has allegiance. He is buoyed by his teams' victories and depressed by their defeats. On some nights he cannot fall asleep after a close game that has ended in a loss or after he has watched a particularly exciting contest.

Things bother him that are, at most, on the periphery of consciousness for most people. He cannot understand, for example, the designated hitter rule or why the NCAA holds no tournament to decide the championship in college football. He exasperates relatives who have limited interest as he explains his perspective and rationale at the annual family Thanksgiving gathering.

He is an unusually superstitious person. He stands on one foot when an opponent is shooting a crucial free throw because on a number of occasions this posture has jinxed players at critical points. Near the end of an NFL playoff game he once forbid the fifteen-year-old daughter of a friend from going to the bathroom because the teenager had been, up until then, seated in a place that he deemed to be a lucky spot.

ESPN has been a godsend for him. Life before SportsCenter seems like a primitive era, akin to a past when one had to live without indoor plumbing or electricity. He would sooner walk barefoot over broken glass than move to an area that did not have cable television. The proliferation of sports on television, with ESPN, ESPN2, the NFL network, and other dedicated sports channels, has made a substantive difference in his life.

When he met a woman on a blind date and she told him she does not understand the big deal made in this country about sports, he knew that the relationship would not launch. He thinks his friend Mark's wife, a Jets fan who wears her "Pennington" jersey every Sunday (even during bye weeks), is a true find. Mark, he often marvels, hit the jackpot.

His refrigerator magnets pin the menus from Chinese restaurants and submarine shops. The schedule for the Boston Red Sox obscures the emergency numbers for the fire and police departments.

He considers that a genuine advantage to living on the West Coast is to be able to watch Sunday football games beginning at 10 a.m.

When he first walked into a Las Vegas Sports Book on the morning of the initial Thursday of the NCAA basketball tournament he felt that he was in heaven.

The Madness of March

I Love Virginia

I'm waiting for my flight to Las Vegas at a long narrow table in an airport bar. A tall, lean fellow is seated to my right. He's wearing navy slacks and a pinstriped button-down shirt. A well-worn suede leather jacket is draped over his chair. He has pushed a half-eaten sandwich away so he can stare at a document in front of him. Every now and again, he takes an absent-minded swig from a beer in a pint glass.

The document he's studying and scribbling on is an NCAA tournament bracket sheet. I engage him and discover, not to my surprise, that he too is going to Las Vegas. We will be taking the same flight this evening. He introduces himself as Buddy. In a short time, he tells me that he does not really "do basketball" in Vegas, but instead spends time on the gaming tables.

"Every year I go meet up with college buddies during March Madness. They're nuts," he says. He waves his right arm forward like he is tossing a crumpled piece of paper into a wastebasket, not pretending to shoot a foul shot, but rather emphasizing his "you can have it" attitude toward his college buddies' habits.

He shakes his head and waves his arm again in the same way.

"They're nuts. I swear they'll watch every single game. Sit in the sports book for twelve straight hours. Only budge to get beer. Occasionally go stuff themselves at a buffet. Forty-eight basketball games. You think I'm kidding? I'm not kidding. I mean, how much basketball can you watch?"

"That's a lot of basketball."

"Sure is. Not for me. I play blackjack."

"Blackjack, eh?"

"Blackjack. Not even going to sleep tonight."

"Not sleeping? What do you mean you are not sleeping?"

"Not sleeping. Get to Vegas and it is time to play blackjack. We land, I grab my bag, go directly to the tables." He waves his arm, this time like a football referee signaling a first down. "Directly to the tables. I'll sleep tomorrow morning. I'm not watching forty-eight basketball games."

I point to the tournament bracket sheet he has been completing.

"Hey," he says, "as long as I'm going, I'll fill them out." Then he pauses a few seconds before asking a question. "You like Virginia?"

"I love Virginia," I say.

• • •

I know very little about handicapping college basketball games. I began traveling to Las Vegas for March Madness in 2001 after hearing about an article that listed a hundred things to do before you die. One of the recommended activities was to visit Las Vegas during the first weekend of the NCAA men's basketball tournament. Then I read a short piece in *Sports Illustrated* that made the same point. I went.

It was, as advertised, a unique experience, entertaining and in its own way fascinating. I skipped the 2002 tournament, but since 2003 I have been visiting Las Vegas annually in March. During my third trip, it crossed my mind that the quirky characters I met on those weekends represented a distinct and intriguing subculture worth studying. Consequently, in the course of enjoying the experience of March Madness as a participant, I became an observer, researcher, and note taker.

I have been a sports enthusiast since childhood. I am old enough to have taped pictures of the 1957 New York Knickerbockers on the bedroom wall. When I was ten, I shook hands, awestruck, with the great Connie Hawkins at a gym in Brooklyn when he was still a senior at Boys High School. As a preteen, I watched Lew Alcindor (now Kareem Abdul-Jabbar) play a preliminary game at the old Madison Square Garden when he was only a freshman at Power Memorial. I've played college basketball on a University of Albany freshman team and coached youngsters in recreational leagues and at summer camp. I may know more about the game than the average person.

As it relates to betting, however, I'm no more of an expert than the common fan, except that I know that I could not be much more of an expert than the common fan. Wagering on most sporting events, the NCAA basketball tournament included, is like betting on the flip of a coin: wisdom, knowledge, and experience are limited assets. Hardly any of the thousands who will be traveling to Las Vegas this weekend to wager on the games know enough about handicapping to do anything other than contribute to the collective wealth of the state of Nevada. They cannot wait to get there to begin making deposits.

I know I know nothing, but nevertheless, I do love Virginia in its first-round game. I tell that to Buddy, my new friend the blackjack player.

"You sure?"

"Run from anyone who tells you he's sure," I say.

He laughs and continues filling out his brackets.

"Vegas is some town," he says with his head down. "Do you know there are still only about seven cab companies that control all the traffic from the airport?"

"No, I did not know that."

"Crazy place," he says. "A lot of the people who go to Vegas, man, are wack jobs." He shakes his head.

"You mean like the kind of guys who play blackjack all night?"

Buddy picks up his head and laughs. "Yeah, maybe I'm a wack job too. But only for one weekend a year. And I'm nothing like my friends the basketball junkies. They're crazy." He pushes his hand forward.

Another man arrives and parks himself at our table. He hails the waitress before his rump hits the chair and shouts for a beer. Twenty-four ounces or sixteen, she wants to know—twenty-four for him.

This man is oozing March Madness. He wears jeans, running shoes, and a blue sweatshirt with "Syracuse" in orange on the front. His baseball cap is turned backward. He's placed an accordionlike file folder on the table space in front of him and, once settled, yanks this morning's *USA Today* out of one of the pockets.

"You going to Las Vegas for the tournament?" I ask, knowing that it is an unnecessary question.

"Every year." He's working on the bracket sheets with a pen.

"Ink?"

He snorts and doesn't look up.

"You seem confident."

Again he snorts and waves dismissively.

"Sorry about Syracuse."

Syracuse, a perennial college basketball power, has not been invited to play in this year's tournament.

"We were screwed," he says. But he doesn't look up from the bracket sheets. He's busy. It's Tuesday. The tournament begins on Thursday.

I swing around on my chair and notice a table of four young men. They're joking and poring over bracket sheets. There's another cluster of three at a table to the right of Buddy. I walk over to them and see that they're jawing over a bracket pullout from *Sports Illustrated*.

•••

On the plane I sit next to a woman who knows nothing about basketball. She finds it amusing, almost astonishing, that people would fly to Las Vegas to watch basketball games. Bewildered, she asks me several questions. She is traveling to a convention for entrepreneurs who sell health-related products. She is also a prolific author and within minutes is aggressively peddling the various unusual books she has written. We're not across the Mississippi before she's sold me one of her books: *How to Have Sex in the Woods*.

•••

It's midnight when we arrive. Despite the hour, there is a long line for people looking for cabs. I meet a young man on the queue who has traveled to Las Vegas so he can attend a bachelor party.

"Your own?" I ask.

"Nah. College buddy. He's not getting married until June but he and the rest of us are all basketball nuts. We figured we'd combine the party with the games."

We talk about the tournament. He tells me he once guarded

Stacey Augmon, a member of a great team from the University of Nevada at Las Vegas.

"It was the year they were undefeated until they lost to Duke in the semis. I played for Long Beach State. We were in their division. They clocked us twice."

"What was that like, guarding Stacey Augmon?"

"Like playing basketball when you were six against your father. Those guys, the good ones, they are in another category of human being. Still it was great. We got spanked, but it was great. Never forget it. I'll never get basketball out of my system. Positive of that."

The conversation ebbs.

"So," he starts up, "you like Texas Tech?"

Near the front of the line we decide to share a cab. A sourpuss of a cabbie heaves our luggage into the trunk and asks for our destinations. Then, without solicitation, he restates what Buddy told me about seven companies owning all the taxis in Las Vegas. He says that an entrepreneur can't start his own fleet. He's not very pleased about this state of affairs.

"Is this right? Is this fair? Is this America?"

• • •

I arrive at my hotel, the Imperial Palace, after 1 a.m. The hotel is on Las Vegas Boulevard—the road commonly referred to as the Strip. The cabbie makes a right into a driveway, follows the drive around to the left, and deposits me by the hotel's main entrance, which is set well back from the Strip. After we settle the tab, the driver will take the man who guarded Stacey Augmon to Treasure Island, a hotel farther north on the Strip. The bill is $18 for the twelve-minute ride. The cabbie suggests it would be a "whole lot less" if there was no monopoly on the taxi industry.

• • •

I check in at the registration counter among more chaos than I expected. The casino commotion reminds me of my previous visits, but it seems more intense than it should be for 1 in the morning. There's also some confusion at the front desk. I had specifically asked for a room that allowed for an Internet connection and am told that my room has none. I politely ask for a change. The attendant says okay but the tone of her voice makes it sound like I'll be sorry. And eventually, I am.

I walk past a set of escalators that I know leads up to the sports book and continue beyond the escalators to an area of blackjack tables with a rock and roll theme. Impersonators of famous singers are dealing blackjack. Elvis Presley is crooning "Teddy Bear" amid the commotion. I go by the blackjack tables, hundreds of slot machines, and two hotel bars before I arrive at the bank of elevators that will take me to my room.

In my reassigned room on the eighteenth floor I find that I can indeed connect to the Internet. However, I can barely hear myself think. It sounds like a band is playing at 1:20 a.m. right outside my window. I open the sliding door that leads to the balcony and discover that a band actually is playing right outside my window. The band continues to blast brass and percussion until 2 a.m. I'm too tired to go downstairs and change rooms. I put a pillow over my head, think about my cabmate playing defense against Stacey Augmon, Buddy playing blackjack downtown, and the Syracuse handicapper who can't look up from his bracket sheets, and do my best to fall asleep.

Jamar Wilson. Jamar Wilson. Jamar Wilson.

At 6 a.m. my cell phone rings. A colleague from back East, washed, dressed, and in his office at 9, has a question for me. I haven't slept for more than four hours since I purchased *How to Have Sex in the Woods*.

After I do my best to answer the question, I ride down to the lobby and ask to have my room changed to the quiet side of the hotel. I wonder if my bloodshot eyes will be a compelling argument but consider the likelihood that bloodshot eyes are not uncommon in these parts. I'm relieved when they accommodate me without a fuss. My new non-laptop-rattling room will be ready by 2.

I know that today will be the first of several long days, but I'm also sure that trying to go back to sleep will be futile and frustrating to boot. So I leave the long registration counter, exit the front of the hotel, and head for the Strip.

The Strip is relatively quiet. Straggling gamblers stumble along the sidewalk, as if they have spent the night, like Buddy, at the gaming tables. It is odd to see early-morning pedestrians carrying beer bottles instead of coffee cups. Employees of the various hotels glumly arrive to punch in at 7 for the day's work. They're just as grim as the plodding gamblers.

I head down the Strip on the Imperial Palace side of the street. One casino follows right after another: O'Sheas, the Flamingo, the Barnaby Coast. A sign on the Barnaby Coast indicates that soon the name will change to Bill's. As soon as I pass the Barnaby Coast I arrive at Flamingo Road, a major intersection on the boulevard.

An intricate elevated walkway at Flamingo Road allows pedestrians to cross either street without danger. Even at this sleepy hour it would be wise to use this overpass. Crossing above Flamingo, I stop and take in the view. Even though I've been here before, the scene is still a marvel.

In front of me rises the massive Bally's, and next to it the faux Eiffel Tower that serves as a landmark for the Paris Hotel. Across the boulevard is the enormously ornate and imposing Caesars Palace complex and then the Bellagio, with its artificial lake and opulent façade.

Beyond the Paris and the Bellagio are the Aladdin and the MGM Grand on one side of the Strip, and the Monte Carlo, New York New York, Excalibur, Luxor, Mandalay Bay, and Tropicana on the other. Every one of these buildings houses thousands of slot machines, hundreds of gaming tables, and multiple bars, restaurants, and theaters.

Turning around on the pedestrian bridge I see just as many hotels and casinos: the Mirage, Treasure Island, Harrah's, Casino Royale, and the Venetian. Casinos and neon lead all the way to downtown Las Vegas, where there are even more establishments. To the uninitiated, the string of flashy and flashing casinos is stunning, especially since beyond the Strip lies nothing but pristine mountains and desert. This boulevard of continuous wildness sits in the middle of nowhere.

I cross Flamingo Road and take the staircase down to the Strip, where a long people-mover walkway, like those at airports, leads to the main hotel entrance to Bally's. Bally's is enormous, with over 2,800 guest rooms and 67,000 square feet of casino floor space. Inside, one flight down on the escalator, the vast casino is buzzing: the roulette wheels, gaming tables, slot machines, retail shops, eateries, and bars are doing a surprisingly good business at 7:40 a.m. It takes me nearly ten minutes to walk the half-mile from the Las Vegas Boulevard entrance to the sports book at the back of the hotel.

•••

The entry to Bally's sports book is through a lounge that is cordoned off from the concourse by a metal railing. Once past the last barstool, patrons turn to the right and find themselves in the rear of a tiered auditorium that seats over 225 customers, plus standing room for those so inclined. The room is designed like a lecture hall. However, bettors—not students—sit behind the long, curved tables that are bolted to the floor. Instead of undergraduates listening to a professor discuss anthropology, those parked in the book—who might, in fact, be undergraduates—watch sporting events on which they are likely to have bet. Five large television screens are suspended from the ceiling of the auditorium, and 210 individually-sized televisions are bolted to the tables so that seated bettors can switch channels at their pleasure to view the games on which they have placed bets. In the adjacent sports bar twenty additional thirty-five-inch television sets are propped up in various locations above and around the bar.

Two ramps lead from the rear of the auditorium to its base, separating the seating area into three sections. At the bottom of the ramps, customers place their bets at counters. A giant electronic scoreboard provides bettors with up-to-the-second information on the betting odds for games that will be played in the next few days, as well as recent game results. Every casino in town has a sports book of one sort or another. Bally's has one of the largest, and during March Madness it is extraordinarily popular.

The sports bar is set up a little differently for the tournament this year. In the past, small round tables that could each accommodate four or five spectators were scattered in an open area beyond the barstools, but this year, several rows of long tables face the television screens, and another set of even longer tables encroach on the walkway that separates the bar from two restaurants. All this seating is in addition to the permanently installed chairs in the sports book proper. Apparently, Bally's anticipates a huge crowd this weekend.

•••

Only two men are seated in the auditorium. Tomorrow at 8 a.m. will be another story—I know from past experience that by tomorrow at 6 a.m. it will be difficult to find open seats. But now the auditorium is empty except for these two. One is asleep, or very nearly so, as he leans forward in his chair in the last row of the room, jerking awake now and again. The other is seated halfway down the ramp along the aisle in the far section of the auditorium, busy making notes.

This is Arnie, from Dallas by way of Trenton, New Jersey. Arnie is the genuine article. He is working on his picks for the weekend and has a loose-leaf binder on the table by his seat. In the notebook is eye-popping detailed information about each of the sixty-four teams in the tournament.

I ask Arnie if he comes to Las Vegas annually for March Madness; he tells me this is his twenty-second year. He continues to explain in more detail. Arnie is caffeinated.

"Came first in eighty-five with a friend. Now there are six of us who meet up here. I missed one year. I was way sick in ninety-eight. Otherwise I would have been here. Believe me. I was way sick."

"Twenty-two years," I say.

"Twenty-two years. Yup." He nods, beaming.

Arnie is effusive about how much he enjoys the weekend and how he looks forward to the party every year. After twenty-two years he still looks like a boy waiting for his birthday present. He has a job in a bank and has never been married. He says that he "likes the scenery in Las Vegas, if you know what I mean." I don't know what time he arrived at Bally's this morning, but he tells me he'll get here at 4:30 tomorrow to ensure a seat.

I ask him who he likes.

He is eager to tell me. He does not like Boston College to cover against Texas Tech. He thinks Bobby Knight is a great coach and his wisdom will make the difference. He ticks off the three reasons why Boston College won't cover the 2½-point spread using his pinky, ring, and middle fingers: "Coaching, coaching, coaching."

The next day Texas Tech will lose to Boston College by 9 points.

Arnie thinks underdog Albany will beat Virginia outright and tells me precisely why. This prediction is also based on three reasons: "Jamar Wilson. Jamar Wilson. Jamar Wilson."

Jamar Wilson is an excellent player and by far the most skilled on Albany's team. But while my guess is that I know far less than Arnie does about college basketball, I am nearly certain that Virginia will easily cover the insufficient 7½-point spread despite Jamar Wilson's prowess. I tell him that.

"Jamar Wilson. Jamar Wilson. Jamar Wilson," he says again. "Too much Jamar Wilson."

Arnie provides some other wisdom, but like everyone else I will meet, he's flipping a coin and pretending that he knows how the air resistance will affect the result. He tells me that he doesn't bet much, maybe $50 a game, which seems like a fair amount to me. He claims that typically when the weekend is over he comes out even, maybe a little better than even.

I ask him if he ever plays parlays.

"Yes, occasionally I do," says Arnie the banker, "but that's because I'm stupid. You never win parlays." This advice doesn't jibe with the advice of other pundits I'll talk with this weekend.

Arnie is having the time of his life talking with me about how he has the time of his life in Las Vegas. He is speedy but very affable, and despite his strong views on the games, he is delightfully self-effacing.

"Hey, what do I know? You know, it doesn't matter really if I win at basketball. I tend to piss any winnings away at the blackjack table at night."

He waves his arm around the sports book and tells me what I already know.

"Now there are three people in here. You know what it is going to be like in here tomorrow at this time? Crazy, man."

I say goodbye to Arnie so I can keep my appointment with Mike Fay, the sports book manager at the Imperial Palace. As I walk up the ramp I see that the nodding fellow has now fully awakened. He's poring over betting sheets and talking to himself.

"Do like Ohio State. Yes I do. Yes I do. They will cover. Lot of lumber, but yes they will cover. Indeed. Central cannot do. Just cannot do. I think so. I think so. Definitely Buckeyes. Feel good about the Buckeyes."

I'm relieved that he's oblivious to my presence.

While I was speaking with Arnie, another man came into the

sports book. He's taken a seat near the rear of the auditorium on the aisle. As I exit, I smile and say hello to him. He gives me a big smile back. He's waiting for tomorrow just like Arnie. In the next days I will be in Bally's sports book seven different times watching basketball games. Every time I am there while a game is being played, this man I smile at now will be sitting in the exact same spot. Just like the sleeper who is now conversing with himself.

The Sports Book and the Tournament

Every major casino on the Strip has a sports book. Nevada is the only state in the United States where one can legally place a wager on a sporting event other than horse racing. Patrons in a sports book can bet on relatively minor events, like arena football and spring training baseball, as well as major college and professional contests in basketball, hockey, football, and baseball. Bettors can also wager on golf tournaments, tennis tournaments like Wimbledon, and boxing matches. If the outcome of a contest is in doubt and there is enough interest, you probably can find a place on the Strip where you can place a bet on some aspect of the game.

In addition to individual events, bettors can also wager on what are called futures. In the same way Wall Street investors attempt to make money speculating on, for example, coffee futures, bettors can try to earn money predicting the future of, for example, the Chicago Bears.

It works like this. A casino will offer separate odds on the likelihood that the Bears will make the playoffs, win its division, get to the Super Bowl, and win the Super Bowl. Prior to the 2006 National Football League season, bettors would have done well to predict an optimistic future for the Chicago Bears: the odds in Las Vegas were 40–1 against the team reaching the Super Bowl.

The Bears, however, did just that. Those who had wagered $10 in August 2006 forecasting that the Bears would go to the Super Bowl in February 2007 were entitled to nearly $400 in February. The winning is "nearly" $400 because the casino takes a cut. This commission, in the parlance of the casino, is called the vigorish, sometimes just referred to as "the vig." The word "vigorish" is derived from a Russian term that means "winnings." Because of the vig the casino can, theoretically, win regardless of who actually wins or loses a sporting event. One can bet on the future in many sports, including football, baseball, hockey, and the NCAA basketball tournament.

• • •

The people like Arnie from Dallas by way of Trenton who will pack Bally's and all the other sports books tomorrow will be betting primarily on individual college basketball games—not on the fate of the Chicago Bears or the likelihood of Ohio State eventually winning the NCAA tournament. What is called "the action" during the next four days will be on the phenomenon that has come to be referred to as March Madness.

At the end of the college basketball season in March, sixty-five teams are invited by a committee to participate in a tournament. The two weakest of the sixty-five teams meet in a play-in game. The winner of this preliminary contest advances, resulting in a field of sixty-four that competes in a single-elimination tournament to decide the national champion. This competition begins annually on the third Thursday in March.

It is very prestigious and lucrative for schools to be invited to participate in the tournament. Determining which teams should be invited is a difficult task and inevitably results in controversy. Some invitations are extended automatically to schools by virtue of the team having been the winner of its individual conference. Most teams are affiliated with a conference, such as the Big Ten, the Colonial Athletic Association, or America East. With one exception—the Ivy League—all of the conferences determine their champion by playing an intraleague tournament at the conclusion of the season. The victor is declared the champion and is invited to the NCAA tournament regardless of whether the committee actually believes that the winner of that league is one of the 65 best teams in the nation. There are 32 conferences in the country, and therefore 32 of the 65 invitations are automatically predetermined.

The remaining invitations are extended to teams that the committee feels are most deserving. A team that had a 25–5 record but played in a weak conference and did not win their conference tournament will probably not be invited to participate. A team that went 19–11 but played in the Big Ten, ACC, PAC 12, or SEC— all powerful conferences—is more likely to be invited. In strong conferences, several schools can be invited to participate.

Since a finite number of bids are extended and since the revenue for those teams and conferences who are invited is considerable, the annual disputes regarding the bids can be contentious. In 2007, Syracuse University, a team that plays in the Big East—a very strong basketball conference—felt that it deserved to participate. When they did not and Old Dominion University, a team that plays in the relatively weak Colonial Athletic Association, did, a good many Syracuse loyalists—as well as the team's coach—believed justice was not done.

The committee not only selects the sixty-five teams but divides them into four regions and ranks them. In each region there are, after the play-in game, sixteen teams ranked 1 through 16 based on the committee's sense of the strength of a team compared to other teams in the region. These rankings are called seeds. For example, in 2007 Ohio State was a 1 seed in its region, indicating that it was perceived as the strongest team in the region, and Central Connecticut was a 16 seed in the same region, indicating that the committee felt it was the weakest team in the region. In the opening round of the tournament, the 1 seeds like Ohio State play their first game against the 16 seeds like Central Connecticut. Similarly, the 2 seeds play the 15 seeds, the 3 seeds play the 14 seeds, and so on.

The chance that any 1 seed would lose to a number 16 seed are infinitesimal. In fact, since the NCAA adopted a sixty-four-team format in 1985, a 16 seed has never defeated a 1 seed. It is very rare for a 15 seed to defeat a 2 or a 14 to defeat a 3. Since this is the case, most of the bets in the tournament are made against something called a "point spread," or simply the "spread" or the "line." The spread is what makes March, in Las Vegas, such entertaining madness.

Spreads, Locks, Dogs, and Laying Lumber

The spread is essentially a handicap given to a weaker team that balances the contestants in a matchup. For example, in the first round of the 2007 tournament, Louisville, a 6 seed, played Stanford, an 11 seed. The oddsmakers believed that Louisville was 6 points stronger than Stanford, making the spread 6 points. Bettors who wagered on Stanford would collect if Stanford won the game, and they would also collect if Stanford lost as long as the margin of defeat was less than the 6-point handicap, or spread. Bettors who wagered on Louisville had to hope not only that Louisville won the game but also that they "covered" the spread by winning by more than 6 points. If Louisville won by exactly 6 points, the result would be a tie, or a "push," and the bets would be returned to the bettors; to prevent this from happening, spreads often contain half points.

If there were no spread, it would not make sense for a casino to take bets on the game since 16 seeds have always lost to 1 seeds. With a spread, there can still be betting action when, for example, powerful 1 seed North Carolina played weak 16 seed Eastern Kentucky, because the spread was 27 points. This is why every sports book on the Strip is a madhouse during the NCAA tournament: more often than not, bettors are excited about the games right up until the end because they're watching to see if a team covers or beats the spread.

The jargon in a sports book can be colorful. A "dog" is an underdog—the team that is receiving a handicap. The "favorite" is the team predicted to win. "Lumber" refers to the amount of points that are being given up by the favorite, and to "lay lumber" is to give up points. For example, betting on North Carolina, a favorite, to beat Eastern Kentucky, a dog, requires "laying a lot of lumber": a North Carolina bettor would have to give 27 points to Eastern Kentucky as a head start before the game even begins. Given the amount of lumber you have to lay, you might consider betting on the dog and not the favorite. If, regardless of the lumber you are laying or because of the points you are getting, you feel that your bet is a sure thing, you have yourself a "lock" or a "gimmee." A bettor might say, "I don't care if I have to lay twenty-seven, North Carolina is a lock. That may be a lot of lumber, but I will not bet on a dog against North Carolina. They always cover. That game is a gimmee."

In addition to betting the games with the spread, a popular bet in the sports book is the over-under. With this wager the oddsmaker predicts how many total points both teams will score. If you wager on the "over," you are betting that the teams will score more than the oddsmaker predicts. If you bet the "under," you are betting that the teams will fall short. For example, in 2007 the over-under on the Davidson–Maryland game was 157 points. The final score would be 82–70, a total of 152 points. A bet on the under was a winner because the combined score was under 157.

To make matters even more chaotic, bets on the spread and over-under can be wagered for the halftime score only. Also, after a half has concluded, a bettor can bet the spread or the over-under (or both) for the second half only. For example, if the first half ends 42–20, an oddsmaker will then predict how many more points will be scored by both teams in the second half and give the spread just for the second half. A bettor might figure that a team that is being walloped in the first half might play more intensely in the second or that the team that is pummeling its opponents in the first half might play its substitutes in the second. For bookmakers, first-half and second-half bets increase the traffic significantly, especially on the first two days of the tournament when sixteen games are played on each day.

•••

Bettors can also wager on what is called the "money line." As opposed to most basketball wagering, when you bet the money line you are betting the odds not for a team to cover, but for the team to win. Since a money line bet is likely to be successful if you wager on the favorite, a winning money line bet pays less for a favorite than a dog. For example, if a money line is 10 to 1, you would have to wager $100 on the favorite in order to win $10, minus the vig. A winning $10 money line bet on the underdog, on the other hand, would win $100, minus the vig. Some games have no money line. Since a 16 seed in the tournament has never beaten a 1 seed, the money line odds in these games would be enormous.

Another popular betting option is called a "parlay" bet. A

parlay is a wager on a combination of games. You might bet a parlay of Ohio State, Louisville, and North Carolina. In order for you to win, all three teams have to cover the spread. The parlays are often presented on betting cards called "teasers." This is an apt name for them. The payoff on a parlay is attractive, but it is very difficult to win. Instead of winning one contest that is essentially betting on a toss of the coin, a bettor must win several such contests. Bettors who consider themselves wise might see several bets as "locks" and be enticed by the jackpot that a winning parlay bet can yield. The result, more often than not, is an addition to the casino's revenue stream.

In addition to all this, some sports books offer what are called "proposition" bets. These are peculiar wagers based on peripheral aspects of the game. For example, will Central Connecticut ever be ahead of Ohio State? What will the over-under be on victories for all those teams invited to the tournament from the Big Ten? Will Stanford take more foul shots than the total rebounds gathered by the top rebounder of Louisville? Some proposition bets cross over from one sport to another. For example, will Tiger Woods have a lower score in the last round of his golf tournament than Eastern Kentucky's point total in its opening-round game?

What with the concurrent activity on spread bets, money line bets, propositions, over-unders, halftime, and second-half wagers, the sports books are bedlams of cheering and grousing. A man screaming "Yes!" all alone for no apparent reason may have won a second-half bet on the under in a game that no longer is a contest for money line or even spread bets. Knowledgeable bettors often try to figure out what such yelps are about, and when they do, they typically smile as they muse on the madness of Las Vegas in March.

Grab It

Before traveling to Las Vegas in March I wrote to each sports book manager on and near the Strip explaining my project and requesting an interview. Mike Fay was one of three managers who agreed to speak with me.

We arranged to meet at the betting counter of the Imperial Palace sports book. When I arrive someone is standing behind the counter who, unlike the other employees, is wearing a sports jacket. This is Mike. Thin and neatly attired in a white dress shirt and dark slacks, he looks to be in his mid-thirties. He tells me that he graduated from Loyola Marymount in the late 1980s and had worked in a variety of capacities in casinos before earning the job of sports book manager at the Imperial Palace.

Like Bally's, the Imperial Palace has a large and loyal contingent of fans who wager and view the games in a facility that looks like a tiered auditorium with a betting counter at its base. Unlike Bally's, the room is smaller and the tiers are much steeper. Customers sitting at the top of the auditorium can look almost directly down at the base of the room. Screens are suspended from the ceiling for easy viewing, and most customers in the sports book have their own individual television sets bolted on a tabletop in front of them.

The spreads and other betting lines at the Imperial Palace are not electronically displayed as they are at other casinos, but are written and revised manually with a grease pencil on a large whiteboard mounted on the wall behind the counter. In addition to the seats in the sports book, the Imperial Palace uses an enormous ballroom area during March Madness to accommodate its basketball-wagering customers, who often dart from the ballroom to the betting queue and back when they want to place a wager. Seating during March Madness on the Strip is at a premium, but you can almost always find a place to sit in the Imperial Palace ballroom.

I talk with Mike in the second row of the nearly vertical auditorium. He is kind and generous with his time. He tells me that March Madness is the wildest period for sports book managers. Super Bowl weekend and New Year's Eve are also hectic times in Las Vegas, but neither creates as frenzied an atmosphere in the sports book. While many bets are placed on the Super Bowl, including even minute aspects of it, the Super Bowl involves only two contestants and one game. During the first weekend of March Madness, sixty-four teams are involved and forty-eight games are played in a four-day period. Since customers bet not only on the entire game but also on halftime results, second-half scoring, and parlays of all varieties, there is action at the betting counters continuously. Add to the mix the regular horse bettors, and March Madness is well beyond wild for those working the book.

"Tomorrow at about noon, four games will be played nearly concurrently. As soon as the half in one game ends, a group of bettors will line up to wager on the second half. Then, minutes later, when the half of another game ends, we will have more bettors coming to the window. Some who are losing the games they've bet at noon begin to bet on the games that will take place at four, or Friday's games. As soon as the matchups for Saturday are determined, then we'll have another group of games that will be wagered on. It's wild here."

Mike describes the March Madness gamblers as fans, not compulsive gamblers. "They know sports but they're not making a living at this." According to Mike, the thousands of bettors who will be arriving today to bet on the games are nothing like hardened professional gamblers.

"This is like a big frat party. A lot of college kids. For the most part the people here are sports fans, just excited about the event and the scene."

He tells me that some hotels attract a distinctive clientele. The Imperial Palace draws many Midwesterners. Consequently, the casino did well in 2006 when Michigan State lost to George Mason University in the first round of the tournament. Money from bettors came in at 40–1 for Michigan State.

"We have a whole group of customers from Michigan State who are loyal to the Imperial Palace. That game looked like a sure winner for them, so we did well that day."

I had forgotten about that game but recalled it immediately when Mike made the reference. Michigan State versus George Mason University had been scheduled for a Friday. The day before—on the Thursday that began March Madness—I was standing on a long betting line at Bally's conversing with a twenty-two-year old college student from George Washington University. I remember asking him if he was on spring break.

"No, spring break is not until next month."

"Well, what are you doing in Las Vegas on a Thursday?"

He smiled, spread his arms wide, and said, "I'm here for this man." Then immediately he pointed toward the scoreboard and commented on the Michigan State spread.

"Check this out. Michigan State giving only four points to George Mason. Are you kidding me? That is unbelievable. Grab it. George Mason plays in the Colonial. The Colonial? Are you kidding me? Grab it. Grab that sucker."

I told him that I had not intended to bet on Friday's games on Thursday.

"Are you kidding? Grab it. That line is only going to go up."

The young man reminded me that a star player for George Mason had been suspended for the game for punching an opponent in the groin during the Colonial Athletic Association conference tournament.

"The nutcracker. Remember? Socked the Hofstra guy in the nuts. He's suspended. The nutcracker is suspended. He's the high scorer and can't play. Michigan State, the Big Ten, against a slug from the Colonial, playing without their high scorer. Laying only four? I mean, this is the lock's lock. Grab it. Grab that sucker. Grab it."

By the time we arrived at the windows the young man had me in a tizzy, so instead of waiting until the next day, not only did I "grab it" but included it as a component of a "can't miss" parlay.

As Mike Fay reminded me, neither I, nor the student from George Washington, nor the legion of Michigan State fans who congregate at the Imperial Palace were wise to have grabbed that sucker. George Mason even without the nutcracker not only covered but defeated Michigan State. This success began an improbable run that resulted in a berth in the semifinals of the tournament.

• • •

According to Mike, the average bet at the Imperial Palace is usually somewhere between $20 and $50. People do not bet a fortune, but they tend to bet on all the games to keep their interest in it. His biggest challenge is simply getting people through the lines so they don't complain about a long wait—or worse—take their bets to another sports book.

"Some bettors know the drill, but many are new to the sports books. They come up to the window and are unsure how to wager so the people at the counter have to explain the process to the customer. We have a good group and we sensitively respond to all questions, but it can take some time."

Mike tells me that he is a fan himself, and if he was not working at the sports book he would be out watching the games in a sports bar somewhere. I mention that I am an Albany alumnus. Along with Arnie from Dallas by way of Trenton, Mike asserts that Albany will do well against Virginia.

I give Mike my card and he welcomes additional contact.

"Not in the next few days, though. The chaos begins very soon."

Steps away from where Mike and I had been seated, two men are huddled at a table. As I walk by, one says to the other, "But Gonzaga is getting one and a half."

Strictly Slots

Lied Library at the University of Nevada at Las Vegas houses the Center for Gaming Studies, which claims to own the world's largest collection of books and periodicals on gambling. The center has closed shelves that preclude browsing, but staff will fetch materials for researchers, as they did for me, and assist anyone—academic, practitioner, media representatives, or those simply inquisitive—who desires to learn about the gaming industry. The head of the center is Dr. David Schwartz. He was not in when I stopped by to visit, so I left my card and a note asking to speak with him by phone sometime later on.

Nearly all fields have specialized journals, and gambling is no exception. The center owns the *Adams Report: Gaming Business Review*; *Buzz Wilson's Players Choice*; back issues of *Blackjack Forum* (it ceased to exist in 2004); *Casino Chronicle*; *Casino Executive*; *Casino World*; *Gambling Times*; *Gaming for Africa*; *Gaming Law Review*; *Gaming Research and Review Journal*; *Gaming Today*; *Horseplayer*; the only two issues ever published of *Jackpot Magazine*; the *Journal of Gambling Behavior*; the *Journal of Gambling Studies*; *Strictly Slots*; *Thoroughbred Times*; and *You Bet*. I review some of the journals and read through sections of books that the librarians are kind enough to bring out to me. As with other

academic publications and trade magazines, some of these publications are intensely focused and in-depth. No aspect of gambling appears to be too esoteric to be examined.

•••

I am fortunate to get a ride back from the campus to the Strip
from a woman who teaches Spanish at UNLV. It is a short but
interesting ride. She is unusually friendly and takes me well out
of her way to deposit me near the Imperial Palace. She speaks
very little English, and my Spanish is limited to what I've re-
tained from my high school years. We struggle, but communicate. Except for her familiarity with the Strip and the location of
my hotel, nothing at all seems to connect her with what tourists
think of when they contemplate Las Vegas. We two are college
professors discussing, as best we can, the nuances of pedagogy.
We might as well be having this talk about professorial life in
Boston or Chicago, except that when she drops me off at an
intersection on the Strip she needs to dodge several men who
appear to be oblivious to vehicular traffic as they study betting
sheets while crossing Flamingo Road. Just before I get out of
the car she goes through a litany of things she has to do before
tomorrow: speak to a child's teacher, deal with an electrician,
phone a realtor about a home she is considering bidding on. As
I wave goodbye it strikes me that the Las Vegas Strip and March
Madness phenomena may seem otherworldly even to most deni-
zens of Las Vegas.

Charlie/Harry/Albany

I return to my new room at the Imperial Palace and check to
make sure I'm not overlooking a bandstand. I'm not. As promised, I'm now in what has been alleged to be the quiet side of

the hotel. I have some doubts that any side of the hotel can be so appropriately named, but at least I won't feel as if I am in a dance hall this evening.

I find a voicemail message from Charlie Martin, another of the sports book managers who agreed to be interviewed. (Per his request, I have changed his name.) Before I set off for the university I'd left a message for him, and he has been kind enough to respond. The problem is that either the sound quality on the voicemail is not as crisp as it could be or this man is difficult to understand. When I listen to the recording, I am nearly certain that he says "This is Harry Martin returning your call." According to a hotel representative, the sports book manager's name is Charlie Martin. I am almost sure that when he wrote back to me his signature was Charlie Martin, but after playing the tape over a few times, it appears as if Charlie is either Harry or prefers to go by Harry.

When I return the call I decide that the wise thing to do is to finesse my uncertainty and ask for Mr. Martin. As it turns out the ploy is not necessary. He picks up on the first ring himself and signals that he is on the horn with a barked, garbled one-word greeting:

"Harry," he blurts, though it sounds as if he is speaking with a cigar in his mouth.

The mystery solved, I say in return, "Hello, Harry."

"Name is Charlie," he says curtly. The tone of the correction is only a notch removed from a rebuke.

I am puzzled and off balance from the start. Perhaps because of my inadvertent offense, Charlie, not Harry, is less friendly as we begin conversing than he had been when he left his voicemail message. After a few moments he becomes warmer, but not much easier to decipher. We talk for a spell on the phone about the same issues I'd covered with Mike Fay. I ask if I might come by before

7 this evening if I have any additional questions. He says that that would be fine as long as I arrive today and not tomorrow.

"Tomorrow is chaos and I will have no time, as in none, to talk with anyone. Tomorrow I'll only be talking to myself."

Considering the effort required to understand what he has been saying, I'm tempted to suggest that sometimes he has been talking to himself while attempting to communicate with me. Nevertheless, I'm able to take away a number of things from the conversation.

The first is that his perspective on March Madness is very similar to Mike Fay's. He was even more emphatic about March Madness being the busiest time of the year, busier even than the Super Bowl. He said that the NCAA tournament's first weekend was "the Super Bowl times three, maybe four." Like Mike, Charlie emphasized that while the Super Bowl might have many bets on parts of the contest, it is still only one game.

"This weekend there will be thirty-two games in two days, forty-eight before Monday. Winners cannot wait to get back on line and win more. Losers cannot wait to get back on line and get back what they lost. Since bettors can bet on halftime and the second half, the action is nonstop. Nonstop. Each game is almost like a Super Bowl. Forty-eight of them. Forty-eight."

Charlie, also like Mike, argued that most bettors during March Madness are not inveterate or compulsive gamblers.

"They're college kids for the most part and adults who never stopped being college kids. They're fans. Sports nuts, plain and simple. I know. I'm one of them. I'd be traveling through the books on the Strip myself if I wasn't working tomorrow."

"You would, eh?"

"Absolutely. Are you kidding? This scene is like a huge street party. Every casino plays host to parading sports junkies who traipse from one hotel to another."

Charlie also made some interesting comments about the value of betting on basketball games. He suggested that people who do their homework can win because so many novice bettors wager on teams because of past years' performances or because of the reputation of the conference, as opposed to a team's inherent talent. Charlie cited a team like Kentucky as an example. He contended that some people will bet on Kentucky because they play in the traditionally strong Southeast Conference and because they, historically, have been good. He said that regardless of who is actually playing for Kentucky, novice bettors will bet on them just because it's Kentucky.

"Five sixty-year-old drunks could be playing for Kentucky and money would still come in for them."

Similarly, small schools—and here he identified Oral Roberts as an example—are not perceived as good simply because so many people have not heard much about them. He suggested that someone who does the research will discover that Kentucky will not beat Villanova in its opening-round game and that Oral Roberts is getting too many points in its contest against Washington State.

"Many people don't bet on the teams, but on an out-of-whack perception of the teams. Someone who knows what's what can do well. Favorites often are laying too much lumber. Smart guys know this."

His argument made sense. Reality, often, cannot compete with perceptions of reality. Those who do not do their own investigation and explore reality settle for a construction of reality based on media representations, history, and rumor. If amateur bettors wager on Kentucky because of its name when the current squad is not as good as past Kentucky teams, the spread on the game will widen, making a bet on Kentucky's opponent an intelligent one.

While Charlie's logic seemed wise to me, the application of it was ironically illogical. It was not so much that the two examples he used to illustrate his point turned out to undermine his contention (a bet on Kentucky turned out to be a winner and one on Oral Roberts a losing one). It was more that Charlie, however knowledgeable, employed the same faulty logic that he attributed to novices.

I asked Charlie if he had any strong feelings on this year's tournament teams and was startled when he told me that he had Albany to beat both Virginia and its likely second-round opponent, Tennessee. When he said this he became the third person who had made such a prediction.

And this, I am as certain as one can be about such matters, will not happen. Charlie's pick is ironic because it illustrates the power and lure of constructed reality, the precise factor that he identified as being the Achilles heel of the wagering public.

If some people possess the wisdom to predict outcomes of sporting events, I am not among this small tribe. I win some and lose some—often winning the games I am least sure of and losing ones that I am most sure that I will win. Nevertheless, I know that the real Albany cannot beat Virginia and will never get to play Tennessee in the second round.

I know this because I am familiar with the real Albany and know that there is a huge discrepancy between it and how the team is perceived. In preparation for this book, and also because it is my alma mater, I followed Albany's basketball team throughout the 2006–2007 season. I watched the games they played at Harvard, Boston University, and the University of New Hampshire. I studied the box scores after every regular-season contest. I attended the first round of the America East tournament and watched every minute of the America East championship game that was televised on ESPN2. I also viewed a number of other

Albany contests that were televised during the season. I chatted with the sports information directors for the America East Conference and the University of Albany. Throughout the year, I met with various members of the media who covered Albany and the America East and was privy to all the printed information about the team that is disseminated to media members who cover the season.

The real Albany has players who play intelligently and are well coached. Jamar Wilson, Arnie's favorite, is especially talented. Several of the other players have been on the team for three years, and the chemistry on the squad appears to be good. However, the team has no real big man presence and has struggled to defeat some weak opponents.

The real Albany was invited to the 2007 tournament because they beat Vermont in the America East championship game by a single point and got an automatic invitation to the tournament. Albany played their hearts out in the Vermont game, but the result was a fluke. A leading scorer for Vermont was injured on the opening tip and then played sporadically and ineffectively during the remainder of the game. Jamar Wilson performed like a whirling magician—but in a way he could not if guarded by stronger opponents. Vermont actually had a chance to win at the end, but a regrettable coaching choice resulted in them not being able to get a shot off before time expired. If you followed Albany throughout the year you knew that in 2006–2007 the team was lucky to have been invited to the tournament.

However, this does not matter to most of the bettors in Las Vegas. They are betting on the construction that has become Albany.

Last year, Albany had a much stronger team, and they easily won the conference championship, gaining its first-ever invitation to the tournament. A 16 seed in its region, Albany played brilliantly in its only March Madness game in 2006 against the stunned 1 seed, University of Connecticut. Connecticut may have assumed they could sleepwalk and beat their notion of Albany, but they almost became the first 1 seed ever to lose to a 16 seed in the tournament. Albany was ahead by double digits with 12 minutes remaining before Connecticut asserted itself and avoided embarrassment. Nevertheless, overnight, among basketball aficionados Albany had become the little engine that almost could.

That was last year. This year the team was not nearly as strong. However, because of its prior success and the attendant media coverage and discourse based on last year, the NCAA committee ranked Albany as a 13 seed. This respect was nice for Albany fans, but not warranted. The respect resulted in wagers placed on this year's Albany team creating a tiny 7½-point spread in its opening-round game against the 4 seed, Virginia. Virginia bettors would not so much have to lay lumber on this game as only a splinter or two.

To bettors, even knowledgeable ones like Charlie Martin, the Albany that was invited to the tournament on a fluke cannot compete with the Albany that almost beat Connecticut on national television last year.

It is possible, like any bettor who is "sure" of something, that my reasoning might prove to be faulty in retrospect. Charlie is the third person who seems knowledgeable and who has argued strongly for Albany. But it doesn't make sense. Charlie argued that the more that you know the wiser you can be when making a bet. But what happens when what you think you know is merely a composite of spurious data? Then your constructions, deductions, and communications are based on a precarious foundation. Then, what you "know"—and by extension what a society or subculture "knows"—actually becomes an impediment to effective decision making. These constructions are particularly insidious impediments because they are dressed up as immutable truths, promulgated in our communications as facts, and consequently can become embedded in our individual and collective consciousness.

How good is Albany? What is Las Vegas? Who are the March Madness bettors? A key to understanding betting, bettors, culture, or anything else is the ability to accurately depict realities and make distinctions between what is real and what are inaccurate constructions.

Of course, the damage related to substituting constructed reality for actual reality has far more problematic repercussions outside the world of sports than inside it. Notions of love, family, and marriage, for example, are really only constructions, conceptualizations advanced by our experiences, communications, and media representations. These constructions can be illusory, spurious, and consequently insidious. Romantic love is, of course, multifaceted and can exist in various forms. Families are complex, and each one is unique. If our conceptions of family and love are based on monolithic constructions, and our families and loves are inconsistent with these notions, we may feel like failures when our relationships are not akin to these constructions of reality. We may even attempt to seek out relationships that conform to the illusion and try to assemble families to meet the constructed reality. The disparity between actual experience and constructed reality can be depressing when these two unrelated entities collide.

In sports and for Charlie, the repercussions of such collisions are relatively trivial. There will be upsets in games, and bettors or casinos may lose some money. These are minor consequences. In fact, an attraction of sports, unlike other aspects of life, is that sports have comparatively fewer abstractions and elusive constructions. Fans and bettors are comforted by the fact they can depend on unwavering realities that are not based on societal or individual constructions. In college basketball a team has 35 seconds to attempt a shot that hits the rim or that team will have to relinquish the ball. This rule does not vary depending on the region, spiritual orientation of the officials, political perspective of the league president, or opinions of sports broadcasters. A clever spokesperson for a team cannot negotiate the shot clock to 40 seconds. The game will have two 20-minute halves, and no one can debate that issue for special circumstances. A fan or bettor can count on players being disqualified once they are charged with a fifth personal foul. In all NCAA tournament games, when the time left in a half drops below 16 minutes a television time-out is called at the first dead ball. These realities are not constructed. The pedigree of a team may be a constructed reality, and that may account for an inappropriate spread in the Albany–Virginia game, but the game itself will hold the interest of the fandom in part because not much else about the game is variable. Yet by extension Arnie, Mike, and Charlie's inaccurate construction of Albany is significant both within and beyond the world of sports. The ability to distinguish what is from what appears to be—especially in an environment with powerful and frequent mediated communications—is a significant determinant of individual and societal success and progress, for Charlie and for everyone else.

•••

Later in the evening I go to Charlie Martin's hotel to talk with him in person. A worker at the sports book counter agrees to locate him for me. A few moments later a very large man appears from behind a curtain in the back. Charlie is all of six feet four inches, three hundred pounds, and is physically imposing in his late twenties or early thirties. I am not surprised when he tells me he played college football.

When he first emerges I wonder if my visit is at an inopportune time—maybe he regretted agreeing to be available when we spoke earlier in the day. Within moments, however, Charlie transforms from dour to affable and effusive. He enjoys talking sports and bookmaking, so much so that I wonder if I will be able to extricate myself in time to watch the end of the Vermont–Kansas State National Invitation Tournament game that is being televised on nearly all the screens in the sports book. The NIT is a second-tier tournament, one that teams who have failed to make the big NCAA dance may be invited to. I mention to Charlie that the game is close and that the decided underdog Vermont is ahead. He shrugs and tells me that Vermont should win outright.

"Like I told you. Nobody hears of Vermont basketball. Kansas State sounds like Kansas. People have heard of Kansas."

Vermont does not win outright. While Vermont covers the spread, they are defeated by 2 points, losers for the second consecutive week when they had an opportunity to take a last shot. This time they took a shot, but it was wildly off target and Kansas State advanced.

I say goodbye to Charlie before the game concludes. I watch Vermont's desperation shot clank away and spot a fellow with a Vermont hat watching as well. He shakes his head.

"I am an alum," he tells me. "Second week in a row we lose in the last second. This is going to be tough to shake." He sounds like he lost a friend in a fire.

Holds and Handles

Doug Worthington (not his real name), the third sports book manager who had agreed to talk with me, phoned my cell in response to an e-mail I had sent him upon my arrival. He said he would be happy to speak with me if I stopped by the betting counter at his hotel. When I arrive a courteous attendant asks me to wait for a few moments. Shortly thereafter Doug comes out to greet me and then takes me back to his office.

Doug Worthington is a handsome five-ten with dark hair and an easy smile. He is in his mid-fifties and has been working and living in Las Vegas for thirty-five years. Originally from the Astoria section of Queens, New York, Doug has New York City memorabilia in his office and a framed photo of Shea Stadium mounted on the wall.

We chat about baseball in New York for a spell. Doug tells me that his father was a New York Giants fan, which is interesting since his mother rooted for the rival Dodgers. Originally a New Yorker myself and of approximately the same vintage as Doug, I know how devoted New Yorkers were to these teams. My understanding of what it meant to be a fan began when I heard passionate arguments as a child about the relative merits of Willie Mays and Duke Snyder that could easily digress into fistfights. I am sure that twenty-five percent of the bettors outside of Doug's office can relay, quite sincerely, stories of brawls fueled by disagreements over the pedigree of one player or another. Doug and I commiserate about the effects that the Giants and Dodgers move to California had on New Yorkers. He tells me that his father eventually forgave the Giants for moving to San Francisco. His mother, however, could never do the same when she considered the Dodgers' flight to Los Angeles.

During his senior year in high school, Doug's family left Queens for Hilton Head, South Carolina. After a short time there, Doug decided that Hilton Head was not where he wanted to be, so in the early seventies he headed west to carve out a niche in the booming city of Las Vegas. He found work in what would appear today to be an archaic-looking sports book. He started as a "board man," the employee who wrote and posted the spreads, odds, and scores on a whiteboard behind a betting counter in the book. Doug continued to progress in the world of Las Vegas to the extent that now he manages one of the more attractive and sophisticated sports books on the Strip.

Doug's office is directly behind the sports book betting counters. In front of his desk are television monitors that display each of the games that are currently projected on the enormous screens outside. Behind him, on a separate table, sits a computer that informs him at any given moment how much is being wagered on which teams, up to the penny. He seems relaxed on this day before March Madness but from our conversation I sense that while he may be relaxed, he has his finger on the pulse of all that is happening.

Doug explains that a sports book wants to make at least seven and a half percent on what is wagered. The total amount bet in a casino is referred to as the "handle," that is, the money they handle. The percentage that the casino retains from the handle is called the "hold." The idea is for the casinos to maximize the hold from their handle. Since most people, he tells me, tend to bet the favorites and the over, the house will realize a greater hold typically if the underdogs and the unders are successful. He affirms what I have heard and read previously in most, but not all, references to the strategy of the house, (see Chad Millman's book *The Odds*, Da Capo, 1991). "I don't care who you bet on, really. It does not matter to me. We'll adjust the spreads as the money comes in to reflect the betting." He implies that if they adjust the spreads wisely they will increase the hold, unless a preponderance of favorites are victorious.

Doug tells me what a student of casino gambling—even a casual student—would realize in a short time. The money made on sports gambling is not as great as the potential for earnings at the casino tables. A bettor who wagers $100 on a basketball game may lose the $100 but will do so in a two-hour period. Even if the player bets the halves it will take an hour for the result to be in. However, a bettor playing blackjack, even one playing at a $10 table, can lose $100 in a matter of minutes. Nevertheless, while most people will lose less betting on basketball than on blackjack, most people must lose wagering on sports, or else the casinos would not support the sports books.

Doug reiterates what the other managers have told me about this weekend. March Madness is one of the busiest, if not the busiest, periods for the sports book. People plan their vacations around the event, and as I had discovered, groups of friends reunite each year in March to watch the games. He said that the crowd the first weekend of the tournament is the most rabid. The forty-eight games have betting on the first half and then the second half, betting the over-under on the whole game and the halves, betting the money line, and betting all forms of parlays. And thousands of people come for the weekend. His handle for the first weekend of the tournament is between $2½ and $3 million. If he realizes the seven and half percent, the Casino gleans about $200,000 during this weekend from the sports book alone.

Doug confirms that the great majority of visitors this weekend are not hardened and incorrigible gamblers, but fans who travel to be with like-minded sports enthusiasts. Estimating conservatively that the average price of a round-trip air ticket to Las Vegas is $200 and the average price of lodging, even split several ways, is at least $200 for four nights—and likely much more—then the cost of traveling to Las Vegas for March Madness is, minimally, about $400 exclusive of food costs. This would mean that if someone traveled to Las Vegas for the purposes of earning money, they would have to expect winnings of more than

$400. Doug estimates that the average bet on a sporting event at his hotel during March Madness is between $100 and $150. Since most people do not win (or could not win, for the sports books to be viable) it is highly unlikely that someone will be able to win $500 betting on basketball games and consequently come out a financial winner for the weekend. It will happen occasionally, but the average person is likely to lose and likely expects to lose. Professional handicappers do not travel anywhere to lose. The people screaming for Central Connecticut to beat the spread are no more vocational gamblers than are regular visitors to Disney World. This weekend is the ultimate outing for sports junkies who, like families who travel to Disney World, are spending what they believe to be expendable income to have a good time.

I asked about the best story he had for me in his thirty-five years. He told me about a character named Crying Joey (not his actual name). Crying Joey came into the casino every Sunday and bet $700 on each professional football game. He was dubbed Crying Joey because as soon as the game began he started whining about the calls, the players, the coaches—complaining about all who could possibly be blamed for apparently conspiring to set him back the $700 he had wagered on each and every game. One day he became so angry that he took off his shoe and threw it at the set. The shoe smashed through the screen and was buried somewhere inside the television.

Silently, Crying Joey walked up to the cashier, peeled off $1,000 in cash for the set, and walked out of the casino with one shoe. Shortly thereafter he came back into the casino—still with one shoe—pulled a chair up to the television, stood on the chair, reached into the set, and grabbed his shoe. He then sat back down on the chair, laced up the shoe, and walked out of the casino.

•••

It is about 8 p.m. when I leave Doug Worthington and his hotel. I walk the several blocks to Bally's. There are more bettors at Bally's at this hour than there had been at Charlie's or Doug's sports book. Several groups are focused, however drunkenly, on an exciting professional basketball game between the Dallas Mavericks and Phoenix Suns. Clusters of others are watching the early rounds of the NIT. I had placed a bet earlier for a friend in the East who is a Hofstra graduate and was getting 10 points wagering on his alma mater in their game against DePaul. The crawl that runs along the base of the television screen says that Hofstra lost by 12, making my buddy a loser.

•••

I ask three men who look to be in their late thirties if I can join them at their table, and they are accommodating. I discover that they are friends who have reunited this weekend to nourish their enthusiasm for the tournament. The conversation is essentially about logistics. They are new to Las Vegas at tournament time and are trying to make some decisions. They ask if I know when they will have to awaken to get a seat in a sports book and about the best venues for viewing the games. I relay my opinion. We then have an extended conversation about beer. They want to know if it is acceptable to buy beer at a convenience store and bring it into a sports book. Debate ensues about the merits and ethics of this. I tell them that in my experience there are no restrictions on hauling beer into a sports book. This seems to relieve the group considerably.

The buddies went to college in California, have kept in touch over the years, and have regularly promised to try out March Madness. One is a teacher, the other is in real estate, and the third is transitioning after a divorce and did not seem to want to discuss his work. Now they are here and ready. One of the three friends now lives in Colorado. He insists that the Air Force Academy, located in Colorado Springs, was mistreated by the selection committee and should have received a bid to the tournament. His friends commiserate. Later in the weekend I see the trio walking down the Strip with a betting sheet and a twelve-pack of beer, apparently discussing an upcoming pick.

•••

I leave the group, wishing them well, and walk around the sports book. One fellow sits with a plastic bag filled with cut-up pears. He's wearing headphones and looks like he is seated in this spot for the long haul and has no intention of abandoning his seat for a night's rest. Against the wall, all the way at the end of a row, is the man I saw sleeping earlier in the day. He too appears to be camping for the evening. Just as he was in the morning, he is nodding in and out of sleep. One of his hands covers a spiral notebook possessively as if concerned that while slumbering some other bettor may come by and escape with the wisdom found in its pages.

•••

The inebriates are really screeching for the Suns in the matchup with the Mavericks. When Steve Nash hits a 3-point field goal to send the game into overtime a group of bettors erupts. During the break a table of boozers diverts their attention to an NIT contest. The group rises as one and gives a standing ovation to a player who approached the foul line and not only missed the shot but failed to hit the rim.

The Suns prevail in double overtime, and afterward the successful bettors march down to the window at Bally's to collect their winnings. The unsuccessful bettors march down to the window to place wagers on tomorrow's contests.

I overhear somewhere that the chances of picking all the brackets are nine quintillion to one.

I leave the squatters and inebriates, cross the Strip, walk into Caesars Palace, and park myself in the sports book to catch the end of the Portland Trail Blazers–Detroit Pistons NBA game.

Twenty-Four-Hour Happy Hour

It is the morning of the first day of the tournament. I wake early, shower, dress, and prepare for the madness that I know awaits me. Before I leave my hotel room I gather what I'll need as I travel through the day. I collect casino betting line sheets, a section of the *New York Daily News* that includes a description of each of the sixty-four teams in the tournament, some pens, and two small yellow notepads. It's 6:30 when I exit the room and walk toward the bank of elevators.

I meet a fellow in the elevator who is from central casting. He is, I discover, a Texan in a long-sleeved baseball T-shirt that has the word "Aggies" written in script across the front. On his head is a Texas A&M cap. He looks to be close to fifty, is nearly six feet tall, and weighs maybe 150 pounds. He has a thick big-buckled belt through his blue jeans, a pen behind one ear, and a toothpick in his mouth. Dangling from his right hand is a spiral notebook stuffed with betting sheets that extend beyond the 8½ by 11 confines of the notebook.

I attempt to start a conversation with him while we ride down to the casino level of the hotel. It is not easy. He seems to be nervous as he anticipates the day. I manage to discover that his name is Denny and that he has been coming to Las Vegas during March Madness for fifteen years with the same group of A&M alums. This year they're staying at the Imperial Palace because they always stay at the Imperial Palace. He tells me that back home he has his own insurance agency. While not unfriendly on the elevator, he is all business, and his business today is not selling insurance. When we reach the casino level, I say goodbye and he grunts something similar as he moves swiftly off the elevator to the sports book.

To get to the Imperial Palace sports book from the lobby elevators you have to pass the celebrity blackjack tables, find the escalators by the registration desk, and take the escalator up one flight to the second level. The sports book is straight ahead behind one of the hotel's bars.

Denny wastes no time once he leaves the elevator. He tucks the notebook under his arm and buzzes ahead like an Olympic race walker, dodges pedestrian traffic that is teetering or otherwise blocking the way, and bolts past Roy Orbison dealing blackjack. I follow at a more moderate pace, feeling like an undercover cop trying to follow a criminal who has a sense he is being tailed and is moving stealthily through the crowd to avoid capture.

I figure Denny is moving so quickly because he believes that an army of fellow gamblers are congregating right now in the sports book and he wants to get on the betting queue before it becomes too long. When I arrive at the top of the escalator I see him immediately. He has not gone into the sports book. He sits slumped against a wall, spiral notebook open, studying the odds on the betting sheets, near, but not at, the end of a line of people waiting for the Imperial Palace ballroom to open. It has over five hundred seats. Almost every patron will be able to obtain a seat in this space. However, Denny, with a Texas A&M hat, Aggies shirt, and a spiral notebook open on his lap, apparently wants to make sure he gets a good spot. Thirty-eight people are ahead of him, and two others are now behind him. It is 6:38. The doors to the ballroom open at 8:45.

"What are you doing?" I ask.

Denny glances up at me then returns his gaze to the betting sheets. "My turn to save seats this year," he says while he makes some notations on a piece of lined paper. His toothpick dances on his lips.

•••

I had decided to watch the first round of games at Bally's, so I leave the Imperial Palace and walk south along the Strip. The pedestrian traffic is heavier than it was yesterday, but still light at this hour. The stumblers are returning from a long night out, but with them are small groups of fast-walking young men I take to be sports bettors hurrying to a casino to make a wager or find a seat to watch the games.

I pass a sign at O'Shea's casino declaring that it has a twenty-four-hour "Happy Hour" policy. This seems to be a peculiar claim, an oxymoron of some sort. If every hour is a happy hour, then no hour can be a distinctively happy one or any more happy than any other. This perplexing semantic issue does not seem to be troubling the nine people who are sitting at O'Shea's bar before 7 enjoying one of the twenty-four happy hours of this day. From the looks of things these people may well have taken advantage of the 6 a.m. and 5 a.m. happy hours at O'Shea's as well. Later in the afternoon and throughout the weekend, O'Shea's has hired a dwarf dressed as a leprechaun to bark outside the tavern, shilling for the casino. Shill or no shill, O'Shea's marketing concept has yielded an appreciative audience.

On the Strip between O'Shea's and the Flamingo I meet a

woman adorned from hat to boots with UCLA paraphernalia. Oversized and adorned with the school's gear she looks like a bear, more like a walking advertisement for UCLA than just a regular fan. When she sees my gaze she says "Go Bruins!" before passing me heading in the other direction.

The Under Is a Lock

At 7:15 a.m. on this first day of the tournament, Bally's sports book is absolutely packed. Chairs—everywhere it seems—are pushed forward, indicating that someone already has the spot. I walk into the bar and feel like someone who has gotten on a crammed subway car and has to maneuver his way to the back by twisting this way and that, bumping others who are either stationary and blocking the path or lumbering in the other direction.

I find a clearing and see a fellow sitting by himself at one of the long tables in the lounge. He has placed items in front of several vacant seats that have been pushed forward. Like Denny, his job apparently is to reserve these spots for his buddies. I find out later that he drew the 5:30 to 8 shift. Another member of his party was parked there from 3 to 5:30 to make sure the group had a good seat for the games. The man on guard now is in his late twenties or early thirties. He is tapping the table with a pencil, nervously waiting for the first game of the tournament to begin. It will not start for two hours and five minutes. He has a loose-leaf notebook with tab separators in front of him, and, in addition to his pencil, felt pens of different colors ready for action. His notebook is filled with information about the teams competing in the tournament. Who is the high scorer? How do they play away from home? What is the average point spread in their games? Do they have any victories against tournament teams?

Bettors elsewhere are poring over the betting sheets and narrow cardboard parlay cards. Across the concourse from the tapping pencil, two men nursing coffee at Johnny's Delicatessen are typical of the norm. They have circled teams on their cards and are discussing their bets.

"Georgetown's laying seventeen points."

"They'll cover."

"I don't know."

"I think they'll cover."

"What about Indiana–Gonzaga?"

"I don't like Gonzaga. They always disappoint. What's the over-under?"

"A hundred forty-two and a half."

"Lotta points. The under, no?"

"Hmm. Does Indiana run?"

"Indiana plays great D. A hundred forty-two and a half? The under is a lock."

"Ok. You're probably right. The under there, but Georgetown laying seventeen? I don't know."

"They'll cover."

"Maybe. Lotta lumber. What about Maryland and Davidson?"

"The ACC is lousy this year."

"Yeah. But Davidson?"

"Maryland is laying seven and a half."

"Wolf got six and a half yesterday at the Bellagio."

"Wolf? When?"

"Yesterday, sometime."

"Fuckin' Wolf. Six and a half would be a lock. What about Weber State?"

And on it goes. These summits are taking place all around me. From nowhere, and not for the first or last time, a stranger materializes and asks, nose to nose, for my opinion.

"Do you like Pitt?"

I am somewhat startled by this abrupt inquiry from someone I've never met and didn't even see coming.

"I don't know. Who do you like?"

"Me," he says, "me, I like Eastern Kentucky. Eastern Kentucky is a lock, Carolina giving twenty-seven and a half? Please. Never cover. That's almost four touchdowns. Eastern Kentucky is a lock, but I've got no sense on Pitt. You know anything about Pitt?"

I apologize and tell him I don't. He tells me it's no problem and wishes me good luck. Then he vanishes as quickly as he appeared.

At 7:20 the ramp leading from the betting counters to the back of the auditorium is jammed with bettors waiting to place a wager. At the base of the ramp, patrons wait on a serpentine line for an available attendant. The line is growing. By 7:30 the space between the last seats in the amphitheater and the rear wall is filled with queued customers jabbering about the wisdom of their bets.

By 8 the line is so long I begin to wonder if I will have time to place a bet before the 9:20 tip-off for the first game.

I Use My System

In front of me on the queue is a man who wears an Ohio State cap. He is about forty or forty-five and has an unlit cigar in his mouth. A huge tropical shirt covers a very big belly and his shorts could fit around a beer keg. The day has not even begun and he is moaning about how he always loses, muttering clichés to anyone who will listen.

"The only luck I have is bad luck," he says.

Then as if someone has said "What did you say?" he again wheezes this announcement, this time in a singsong staccato fashion.

"The-only-luck-I-have . . . is-bad-luck."

I interrupt his whimpering by tapping the back of his shoulder. He turns halfway around and I point to his cap. I remark that he cannot go wrong with Ohio State.

"I can go wrong," he asserts peremptorily. "Believe me, I can go wrong."

He waves his arm to refer to the packed auditorium and by extension all the people at all the casinos at this moment.

"I must be the only guy in Cleveland who comes here and loses money. The only one. Everyone else brags they win, but not me."

He bends his head down and leans into me as if he is about to confide a secret. He starts poking at me with a finger. His cigar breath is horrible.

"What they do is tell you when they win—but leave out all the times they lost." Then he slowly leans back upright and I'm spared another whiff.

"That's what happens. But me, forget about it, the only luck I have is bad luck. The-only-luck-I-have-is-bad-luck."

He mutters this refrain again and again as he continues to wait on the line that nobody is compelling him to be on to bet on games that he contends he knows he will lose.

Another man on the queue laughs at Ohio State's pessimism. He attends Salisbury State University in Maryland. He is thin, maybe twenty-three, and tall enough to make me wonder if he ever played.

"Just in high school," he says. "Didn't start."

Cleveland and I ask about his picks. Specifically we want to know about the Maryland–Davidson game. He tells us that he stays away from Maryland.

"Don't like to bet on the team I root for. With other games I use my system."

An uncle of mine once heard my brother talk about a system he had for betting on blackjack. When my brother finished explaining its nuances, my uncle nodded several times. Then he offered his insight on this matter. "Young man," he remarked, "they send limousines for guys who have systems."

I smile at the recollection but nevertheless am engaged by the college kid's plan.

"I bet fifty dollars on three teams that I know are locks and then twenty-five dollars on a parlay with the same three teams. What always happens, or what usually happens—never say always, right?—is that I win two out of the three games I play in a parlay. So, if I continue to hit two out of the three games in a parlay, but in addition to the parlay bet each game individually, I can't miss."

"Can't miss" are two words I'll hear more than twenty times in the five days I am in Las Vegas. I believe that those two words built many of the hotels on the Strip.

Salisbury State continues to explain his strategy. "If you score with all three in any parlay of the day, you do great. Can't miss."

"You wanna miss," says Ohio State, "let me pick the three for you."

"So who are your three locks?" I ask.

"Not sure yet," Salisbury State responds with a self-effacing smile. "Still working on it."

By the time we get to the counter he has convinced me that the system will work. However, I bet only $10 on each "lock" and $5 on the parlay. Some books will not accept a $5 bet, but Bally's is not one of them. I place my wagers with confidence, feeling pretty good about the system.

Bally's is so crowded that I cannot find a single seat. I spot Arnie with his crew busily handicapping the games and wave hello. Mr. Pears and the sleepyhead are in their seats. The man with the smile is also parked and ready for action. I see no seat for me.

Top of the Morning

I walk through Bally's to the connected Paris Hotel. Many of the hotels in Las Vegas have a distinctive theme, and the Paris has a predictable motif. The signs are in French, the food is something akin to French cuisine, and the support staff are attired in what someone believes to be typically Parisian garments. A huge Eiffel Tower rises from the base of the hotel to well beyond the roof.

Like the Imperial Palace and Bally's, the sports book at the Paris has a tiered auditorium look. However, the rows are not nearly as steeply angled, and the entire sports book area is much smaller than that of either of the other hotels. Wagering patrons queue up along the right side of the room as they wait for an available agent. High along this same wall, game scores and current odds are posted on a large electronic scoreboard. Large screens are suspended from the ceiling, and several television sets are embedded on the front wall above the betting counter.

As is the case in Bally's, patrons access the sports book at the Paris by walking directly through a lounge. The lounge is in itself a sports bar where all the games are displayed on televisions set up on nearly every inch of space along the perimeter of the bar. By the time I arrive, the sports book proper is packed, but there are still some seats at the bar. I find an open stool at about 8:45 a.m.

My can't miss parlay includes Boston College minus 2½ over Texas Tech, Butler minus 2 over Old Dominion, and Texas A&M minus 13 against the University of Pennsylvania. The last of these three wagers was inspired by a man I met on an elevator at 6:30 who was rushing to wait in line for a chair to a room that has nearly unlimited seating and that would not open its door for two hours.

I sit at this Paris bar at 8:45 and prepare to wait the thirty-five minutes for the games to begin. While it is very early, and if at home I might still be brushing my teeth or stumbling in the living room with a cup of coffee, nothing seems inappropriate in this environment about having a cold beer at this hour. In fact, drinking beer seems like the absolutely right thing to do right now in the Paris sports book. Several others seated around the bar have already begun knocking them back. One fellow with a Notre Dame T-shirt hoists his bottle to make a toast. He says to all:

"Eight forty-five a.m. Top of the morning."

Everyone at the bar gets a charge out of the toast, and a number of us join in on a chorus, chanting "Top of the Morning" again. We bang down our beers while pancake houses from Seattle to San Diego are at the peak of their breakfast rush.

Johnny the Virgin

The man seated next to me is a giddy, giggling college student from Austin, Texas. Clearly, he is tickled to be here for the beginning of March Madness. His team, the University of Texas Longhorns, is a 1 seed and will be playing tomorrow afternoon. This is Johnny's first time to Vegas during March Madness.

"Who do you like?" I ask.

Johnny shows me his betting slip. He has bet $20 on a parlay teaser card and selected seven teams. Apparently, he likes Butler, Maryland, Duke, Pitt, BC, Georgetown, and North Carolina.

I roll my eyes at his card. I remember doing this the first time I was in Las Vegas. The teaser cards offer 70–1 odds for a seven-team parlay. This means that if you are successful with all seven wagers on a $20-dollar bet, you walk away with $1,400. It appears to be a good deal.

However, Johnny from Austin might as well take his $20 and put a match to it. It is nearly impossible to win seven games against the spread. It is almost as unlikely as taking a coin, flipping it seven times and getting heads with each toss. I try to explain why it is a difficult bet. He is not distressed and rather gets a joyful kick out of it all.

"This place is great," he comments after I have explained how he has thrown $20 out the window.

At 9:15 as CBS begins its coverage minutes before the opening tip of the Maryland–Davidson game—the first of the forty-eight that thousands will be watching this weekend—everyone at the bar stands up and starts applauding. The Notre Dame fan waits for the applause to subside, rubs his hands together in glee, and booms to us all, "Gentlemen, start your engines."

824 for $50

The sports book is only a few feet from the edge of the bar. I want to explore the scene inside the facility, so I ask Johnny to save my seat. In the book I am collared by a couple who look to be in their fifties. They are from Ohio and want to bet $50 on Ohio State but are unsure of how to read the betting sheets. I provide a brief tutorial.

For March Madness wagering, the words "College Basketball" appear on top of the 8½ by 14 betting sheets in something akin to sixteen-point type. What a bettor sees beneath the heading is information pertaining to the time of the game, spread, over-under points, and money line if there is one. For any contest, each team is assigned a unique number. On the sheet in front of this couple, the number 824 has been assigned to Ohio State. Ohio State is listed as giving 22½ points in the game to Central

Connecticut. In order to place a wager at the counter, a bettor would announce the amount of the bet and the number of the team. So, I tell the couple from Ohio State to say, "Fifty dollars on eight-twenty-four."

The woman repeats my instructions. "I want to bet on eight-twenty-four for fifty dollars."

"Yes." I start to explain the over-under to her, but she puts up her hand like a traffic cop saying in essence. "This is all I want to know."

I want to make sure she gets the concept of the spread. "Do you realize that Ohio State has to win by twenty-three points for you to win?" I ask.

"They do?" she exclaims incredulously. "Why? They have to win by twenty-three points?"

I begin to explain how it works. Again, she puts up her hand.

"Never mind," she says. "This is fun. Eight-twenty-four for fifty dollars! Right?"

"Right."

Don't Mess with the Bulldogs

I wander back into the bar and see a man decked out in Butler gear. He has a Butler hat, a Butler shirt, and wears a pair of nylon wind pants that reads "Butler" under the left hip. Mr. Butler lives in Indiana and, I discover, is a bona fide expert on the Bulldogs. He must be close to sixty years old. I introduce myself and we begin to chat. He tells me, as so many already have, that he travels annually to Las Vegas and meets up with cronies to watch the games. He reminds me that Butler went to the Sweet Sixteen in 2003, winning their initial game on a thrilling last-second shot. He knows the player who made the shot.

"Brandon Miller, now an assistant coach."

He knows the opponent.

"Mississippi State, a five seed."

And he knows the precise final score.

"Forty seven–forty-six. A helluva game."

He also reminds me that in 2001 Butler had drubbed Wake Forest so badly that television cuts to the opposing coach during the first half provided images of someone who appeared to be staring in disbelief—for twenty consecutive minutes—like a man who has stumbled into his living room in the morning and found all the furniture missing.

"Score was forty-three–ten at the half," the Butler alum tells me, still smiling at the six-year-old recollection.

"Also, don't forget we beat Louisville after we beat Mississippi State in oh-three. By eight. Seventy-nine–seventy-one. Louisville was a four seed."

The man knows his Butler.

By this time in our conversation other Butler fans have taken seats at the table that Mr. Bulldog has saved for them. I shake hands with each one. Each one seems to have a Butler story for me. Now I listen to four experts talking all Butler all the time.

"I have Butler minus two against Old Dominion," I say. "What do you think?"

"I think you really may be a college professor," says a Bulldog.

I wave goodbye to return to my seat next to Johnny the Virgin at the bar.

"Don't mess with the Bulldogs!" someone shouts to me as I walk back to my bar stool.

Hi-De-Ho

Only seconds are left in the first half of the game between Boston College and Texas Tech. The two teams are tied. Amid the fans chaotically screaming for Davidson, Maryland, Stanford, and Louisville, a man standing on the periphery of the bar is banging on a metal barrier that separates the bar from the walkway beyond it. He is swearing profusely and pleading for Boston College to take a shot. His banging can be heard despite the regular bellowing of commentary such as "You suck!" "Jesus Christ!" "You gotta be fucking kidding me!" and "Give me a break!"

His hands now tightly grasping the metal railing, the man bounces up and down on his toes. "Take a goddamn shot!" he screams.

Boston College waits for the final seconds of the half, drives the ball to the goal, but misses an easy layup. The man at the rail throws his hands upward, moans, and reels backward as if he's been hit with a dart. Then he slams his hands down again on the railing.

Boston College fights for the rebound, gains possession of the ball, and attempts another shot. As the halftime buzzer sounds, the ball hits every bit of the rim before going through, giving Boston College what might appear to be a relatively insignificant 2-point halftime advantage.

It is not relatively insignificant everywhere. Joy erupts at the railing.

"Hi-De Hi-De-Ho. Yes. Yes. Oh yes. Oh very yes. Very yes. Very much yes. Yes indeed. Hi-De-Ho."

The man at the railing is now ecstatic. He does a bit of a squat, makes a fist with his right hand, and extends his arm. Then he yanks the clenched fist toward him like he's pulling a cord to start a lawn mower.

"All right!" he booms.

He pops up from his near-squatting position and does a bit of a skip and dance step. He sounds like Cab Calloway as he begins to sing a version of "Hi-De-Ho."

"Hi-De Hi-De-Ho. Hi-De-Ho. Hi-De Hi-De-Ho."

"What is that all about?" asks Johnny the Virgin.

I am not sure myself, so I glance at the betting sheets and see that the halftime spread in the game is Boston College minus 1½ points. The last-second Boston College shot that hit every part of the rim before dropping resulted in Boston College leading by 2 at the half. Al Skinner, the BC coach, barely registered any joy, but the made basket is cause for a singing celebration by Mr. Hi-De-Ho. He can do the arithmetic. Subtract 1½ from 2, and a bettor for Boston College in the first half wins by ½ point. This is clearly something that Hi-De-Ho is aware of as he skips, hops, and sings all the way down the ramp to collect his first-half winnings.

•••

Two knockout women who are called "Miller Girls" are passing out T-shirts. They are stunning. I would have loved to have been there for the interview when they applied for the job. Their task, apparently, is to hand out free Miller T-shirts to anyone who is drinking or who promises to drink Miller beer. They are extraordinarily friendly to the men at the bar. As I look around it sure seems that many of my fellow boozers have switched to drinking a Miller product. I suspect that what caused the reversal in brand loyalty had little to do with any sudden awareness of distinctive beer flavor. Austin and I had not been drinking Miller, but we signal the Miller Girls who come by our barstools.

"Do you fellows promise to drink Miller today?"

Austin promises as if he is swearing to respect them in the morning. The girls give us the T-shirts and tell Austin that they "bet he is extra large." Austin grabs the shirt, wheels around to the bartender, and demands a Miller Lite. Then he looks to me as if to say, "Is this heaven or what?"

Things are not going as well for the toastmaster from Notre Dame. He is far glummer than he was at 9 a.m. He mutters, "Two hundred dollars, poof."

Austin's seven-team parlay was history before it began, but now it is officially a loser. Nevertheless, he does not seem to mind a bit as he fondles his new T-shirt.

Despite being in heaven I decide to leave the Paris and watch the noon games at the Imperial Palace. Austin cannot believe I am leaving. He is truly amazed.

"Where are you going, Al? Are you crazy? We are right here, Al. The T-shirts? Are you crazy?"

Nevertheless I leave Austin speechless and wave goodbye to Butler and Notre Dame and the rest of the consumers who began imbibing at 8:45 in the morning. I walk through Bally's casino, take the moving walkway to the Strip, go past the Flamingo and O'Shea's, and enter the Imperial Palace.

When I passed the Flamingo I saw a man holding a betting sheet and ignoring, at his peril, all pedestrian traffic. He was wearing a T-shirt that seemed appropriate. It read, "I can ignore you as long as it takes."

Wright State Did Not Come Here to Lose

So far the system I am following that was designed by the undergraduate at Salisbury State who is probably cutting his classes this week is working well for me. Boston College defeated Texas Tech 84–75. Since I only was laying 2½, I have won the first of the three games I need to complete my parlay. I need Butler to beat Old Dominion by 2, and this should be no problem because the table of rabid Bulldog supporters at the Paris assured me that this bet was a lock. Also, Texas A&M must defeat Pennsylvania by 13. According to Denny, who owns his own insurance agency and rushed at 6:30 to obtain a seat for a 9:20 game in a room with unlimited seating, this wager should also be a sure thing.

I'm in the very steep theater at the Imperial Palace sports book. The lower rows, where I met with Mike Fay yesterday, have been reserved for the regular horse bettors. These dedicated horse folk seem, at best, to be disinterested in the basketball tournament and, at worst, annoyed by the locusts of amateurs who have descended for these four days and really do not understand the etiquette. Some of the basketball bettors are also dabbling with the horses, so throughout the many tiers in the Palace one hears intermittent yelps urging "Groucho" or the "Number Five" to "C'mon!" as the horses near a finish line. "C'mon Groucho. Go Groucho. Go. Go. Go Groucho. C'mon."

I find a seat near the top of the auditorium. The angle is so severe that it seems as if I am looking straight down at the base of the theater. The chair next to me is vacant but newspapers are strewn on the table in front of it. The words THIS SEAT TAKEN have been scrawled on the back of a betting sheet and placed on top of the newspapers. A half hour passes with no one claiming the chair, so when a young kid arrives and asks me if anyone is sitting in the vacant seat I tell him I have not seen anyone. The newcomer parks himself and within minutes a large man with a sizeable beer gut and a white beard comes up the aisle and looms over him. The kid mumbles "Sorry" and vacates. The large man sits down shaking his head and mutters, "Son of a bitch can't read." Then he looks at me, makes a face, and shakes his head again, hoping, I imagine, to elicit some sympathy from me. He seems to be saying, "Can you believe what I have to deal with here?"

I begin to chat with him. Edwin tells me he travels to Las Vegas several times a year from his home in Raleigh, North Carolina.

"Super Bowl, March Madness, a couple of other times. I'm

here a lot." Edwin stops responding long enough to take a swig from a very large plastic travel mug. Then he continues.

"The only thing crazier than this weekend is Super Bowl weekend. You would not believe that."

"Really?" I say.

"Really. Really." Edwin pauses. He turns away from me and puts on a set of reading glasses. He begins to scour horse betting sheets that lie amid the mess of newspapers in front of him. I think our conversation is over when suddenly, without looking up, Edwin resumes his commentary on the Super Bowl.

"People bet on everything during Super Bowl. They bet first quarter, second quarter, over-under on pass completions, over-under on fumbles, over-under on yards gained by everyone who can carry the ball. Proposition bets." He looks up from the papers, removes the specs, and stares at me. "Crazy bullshit proposition bets."

"Crazy bets, huh? Like what?"

"Like what? Okay." He pauses for a second. "Here's a like what. Like, for instance, will the Bears' quarterback—what the hell was his name . . .?" He waves a finger around in circles while trying to recall the name. He can't, but continues nevertheless.

"Whatever the hell his name was—Will the Bears' quarterback have more interceptions than Peyton Manning had in his last three games? That's a like what. Will Marvin Harrison score more touchdowns than the Colts have illegal procedure penalties? That's a like what. Will there be a field goal attempted before the first coach's challenge?" He smirks. "I'm telling you. It's fucking nuts." Then Edwin waves his hand dismissively.

"But the Super Bowl, you can have it."

"Why is that?"

"Only one game. Only one game. This—March Madness—this I would not miss. Sixteen games today alone. I have not missed March Madness in ten years."

"Since ninety-seven?"

"Since ninety-seven. Haven't missed a year." He snaps his fingers and slams the countertop, sending a plastic coffee lid soaring like a tiddly wink. "Grossman!"

"Grossman?"

"Grossman. That was the piece of shit quarterback for the Bears in the Super Bowl. I knew they had no chance with him. Did well on that game. Very well."

I want to know where he works where he can get this time off.

"I work for the state. I have sick time stacked up to here," he says, pointing to a spot a foot over his head. "It's a good job."

He begins to pontificate about his betting prowess. Edwin is remarkably full of himself. He speaks with a certainty that reflects not only a fundamental confidence in his wisdom but also his inability to understand how everyone else could be so foolish.

He tells me he has bet Wright State on the money line against Pittsburgh. Wright State is a 10-point dog. I ask him why he would bet them on the money line.

"Hey," he says. "Wright State doesn't care about the spread. You think Wright State cares about the spread? Wright State doesn't care about the spread."

He pauses again for effect, then leans over to me. "They came here to win!" he asserts, banging out the word "win." "Not to beat the spread." Edwin reaches behind himself with his right hand. He grabs a betting sheet while still leaning toward me. He takes a look at the sheet, then picks his head up with a smile as if he has just discovered something that none of the other dopes in the sports book has realized. "Wright State is paying five to one." Edwin makes a face. "Five to one. Are you kidding? That's a hundred on my twenty."

Then he returns to a ninety-degree sitting position and spreads his arms wide, as if his logic is self-evident and go figure why the other idiots in the sports book do not get it.

While the reasoning doesn't seem unsound to me when I first hear it, it makes less sense when I consider that all teams are playing to win and not against the spread. There will be, at the end of the weekend, forty-eight teams that aspired to win and will have lost, so I am skeptical as I mull over the strategy.

Bearded Edwin continues to expound and explain his theory. Again he leans over to me conspiratorially. "They don't come here to lose." Then he slowly leans back to a normal sitting position, nods, and gives me a wink.

Edwin slaps the table and pops up. "Got a horse I like," he wheezes and bounds away, as much as a man with a belly like his can bound. Throughout the afternoon he pops up and bounds away countless times. All told, the genius is probably in his "This seat taken" spot for no more than thirty minutes.

Later in the day Wright State would, in fact, be pummeled by Pittsburgh despite trying to win the game. It is unfortunate that at that time I was elsewhere because I would have loved to hear Edwin's explanation for this bizarre turn of events.

Take a Knee. Lose Like a Man.

As matters unfold, winning my parlay remains a real possibility. But it will not be easy. I still need Butler and Texas A&M to cover. Old Dominion is gagging against Butler, taking care of one of these problems and making sages of the Bulldog faithful at the Paris. The Texas A&M game, however, is dicey despite Denny's enthusiasm for the Aggies. A&M's opponent is the University of Pennsylvania Quakers, the tournament representative from the relatively weak Ivy League. Down at halftime, the Quakers storm back and actually go ahead of A&M 39–37 in the second half. This is a painful comeback for many in the amphitheater.

I cannot see him, but I am certain that in the ballroom a certain insurance agent is moving his toothpick about at a rapid clip.

To the delight of all those who have bet on A&M, the Aggies recover quickly and surge ahead. But they cannot simply win. They must win by 13½ points for their supporters to be winners. With 33 seconds to play, A&M leads by 16 and Penn has the ball.

Penn has nothing to gain by taking a shot. They will lose regardless of any successful attempt. However, if Penn should make a 3-point field goal, the difference between the winner and loser would be 13 points, and my parlay would go belly up. It seems that several people in this auditorium have made similar wagers and have similar concerns. As Penn prepares to take a final shot that could deplete the savings of many in the Imperial Palace, a man from the back of the auditorium gets up and roars, "TAKE A KNEE!"

Penn does not respond to this request. They take a shot, but they miss. With 23 seconds remaining, A&M retrieves the missed attempt. The scoring differential, to the delight of many in this very steep amphitheater, is still 16.

At this point in a game the team losing will often foul the opponent, stopping the clock and forcing the opponent to make free throws. If the opponent misses them, the losing team can have another opportunity to score and remain alive in the contest. However, when a team is down by 16 points with 23 seconds left, this tactic is valueless because the losing team has no real chance to come back and win from so far behind. Nevertheless, some teams will continue to foul even under these hopeless circumstances. In an attempt to discourage such an action from any University of Pennsylvania Quaker, a bettor from the top of the amphitheater screeches at the top of his lungs, "LOSE LIKE A MAN!"

Apparently, the Pennsylvania Quakers intend to do just that.

They do not foul and lose like a man as Texas A&M dribbles away the time left on the clock. I am a winner of all three of my initial wagers and victorious in the parlay. The system has worked! The truant from Salisbury State University I met on the line at Bally's appears to be a genius.

This success, however, is the type that Las Vegas casino owners desire because it breeds hope. It makes bettors think that this can be done regularly. I bet parlays throughout the weekend, employing a modification of the system that the kid from Salisbury State suggested. The early win this afternoon is the only time it works in the four-day period.

As if to offset my euphoria, a quiet fellow to my left with a Cubs hat on is moping. His bald, hatless buddy is also moping. Both are from Chicago and both, as I discover, have not done well this morning. The duo have bet the under on the two games that finished with the over, and the over on the two games that finished with the under.

"Way to go," Cubs Hat says to me without enthusiasm or sarcasm. It is a genuine attempt to congratulate me.

I tell him I am sorry for his losses.

He shakes his head sadly from side to side. His buddy is nodding sadly up and down. It looks almost comical, the heads moving in opposite directions but sending the same message.

"We bet the over," says Up and Down.

"And it comes in the under," says Side to Side.

"We bet the under."

"And it comes in the over."

I tell them again I'm sorry. They wave it off.

"Happens," says Side to Side. "Who do you like tonight?"

I tell him I like Xavier to beat Brigham Young University.

"I'll put some dough down for you on Xavier," he says, as if trying to show his appreciation for my sympathy.

Barely clad waitresses come around asking each person in the auditorium if they want something to drink. The scene is fantastic. Armies of men either glum or euphoric occasionally stare up at women who are either strikingly well endowed or are employing some leverage to make them seem so. The outfits are so stunningly revealing that no one, no matter how discreet or disinterested or ancient or prudish, could avoid gaping at these women.

Up and Down and Side to Side are in their late thirties. They are still bobbing and weaving rhythmically when one of the waitresses comes by.

"Cocktails?" she asks.

This is not an unfamiliar drill, but Up and Down and Side to Side nevertheless stare right at the cleavage of this young woman as they request a beer.

"Not entirely a waste," says Up and Down after the waitress moves beyond our row.

The Vanderbilt–George Washington game is lopsided. Vanderbilt wins by 33 points and only had to cover 3½. Four idiots from Vanderbilt well into inebriation are seated in front of us. They are making fun of George Washington in the first half, shouting for their school and mocking the opponents. They leave halfway through the second half. As they depart one of them barks, "I don't want to spend any more time with these jerks," which is precisely the thought that goes through my mind as they are descending into the pit of the sports book.

Nine Deep

I am in the Imperial Palace ballroom right before the Michigan State game is about to begin at 4:20. This is the room outside of which Denny waited on line for two and half hours before a tip-off in order to get a seat. I couldn't throw a basketball from one side of this room to the other, and I don't think Michael Jordan could either.

Close to sixty tables are set up in here. Each table is covered with a white cloth, and at its center are a bucket of pretzels and a bucket of popcorn donated by the house. As many as ten bettors sit around each table typically clustered in groups of three or four. Sometimes a large group of loyalists will commandeer an entire table or several tables.

The crowd in the ballroom is almost entirely male. The room is noisy, rowdy, and profane. Large television sets, forty feet apart, line the walls. Below each set is a sheet of paper listing the games that will appear on that set during the day. Fans like Denny might be excused for waiting in line so long because they want to get a seat directly in front of a particular set that will show a particular game. Truth is, several sets in the ballroom carry the same game, and from almost anyplace in the hall you can watch almost any game.

In the rear of the hall situated between televisions are two portable minibars. No small amount of beer is being consumed in the Imperial Palace ballroom. Before the Michigan State–Marquette game the line is nine deep at the portable bars. Only two tables in the ballroom are not littered with empty bottles. The boys in this room like their beer.

Directly in front of one of the television sets is a table surrounded by ten Michigan State fans who are preparing to root for their team to beat Marquette—by at least 2 points. Right before tip-off these men, who look to be alums in their early forties, stand up in unison as if on cue from some imagined pep squad director. Boisterously, these adults break into the Michigan State fight song. It concludes with fists pumping in the air to the words "Rah, rah, rah." The group then sits down laughing. They slap high fives with each other, reach for their beers, and settle in for the game.

There are two tables of dedicated Duke rooters in the Imperial Palace this afternoon. From the cheering or despairing sounds emitted throughout the ballroom many more Blue Devil fans are interspersed throughout. The Dukies, poised and ready to scream for the Blue Devils, need not only a victory, but they must defeat the champions of the Colonial Conference—Virginia Commonwealth University—by 8 points.

An Ohio State contingent, dressed in Buckeye scarlet, has congregated in front of a set near the rear of the hall that will be showing Ohio State versus Central Connecticut. Winning will not be an issue for the 1-seeded Buckeyes. These fans, however, need a victory by at least 23 points.

The large woman I saw during my morning stroll wearing UCLA from head to foot is also in the house with a legion of others hoping that their Bruins can defeat Weber State by 20. She is a true fan and not a bettor. She spends time before the game working the room, asking if spectators would be willing to hold or wear Bruin paraphernalia for luck. Her influence must have had an effect as the Bruins eventually win and cover, trouncing Weber State by 28.

The Duke fans are not similarly satisfied. Inexplicably Virginia Commonwealth University, a team from the perceived-to-be-weak Colonial, not only covers but beats Duke on the money line. Edwin must be pleased. Apparently, Virginia Commonwealth did not come here to lose. The Duke upset sends the tables of supporters into a funk that induces them to march to the portable bar in a comical single file. Each fan seems to be shaking his head and trying to make sense out of the defeat.

Breakfast and Margaritas

I decide to leave the Imperial Palace ballroom at halftime of the four o'clock games and move on to the Venetian for the rest of the night's slate. I leave the packed, rowdy ballroom and descend the escalators to the packed, rowdy casino level. At the registration counter, a queue of about ten tourists waits to check in. Outside the building, a long line of people wait by the curb for a cab. It is a Thursday at 5 p.m. in the middle of March, and this city is teeming like Mardi Gras in New Orleans. Fortunately I don't need a cab. The Venetian is a short walk, and besides I want to observe the pedestrian traffic.

The Strip is swarming. Past the Imperial Palace, the sidewalk juts away from the boulevard and takes a turn into an outdoor mall that leads to the Venetian. Retailers have set up carts and booths peddling touristy items to the constant flow of pedestrians. One hawker is attempting, successfully, to convince would-be bikers to sit on a stationary Harley. For a fee the peddler will run a videotape of a moving road while the customers are perched on the bikes, pretending to steer the vehicle. The stationary bikers will take home a video that makes them into something akin to Hell's Angels. Each time I walk by this booth over the weekend people wait in line to ride the Harley.

Halfway around this circular path I am confronted head-on with the miserable bandstand that was the platform for the sounds that exploded into my room during my first night here. At 5:30 this evening, the same cacophony passing for music is blasting onto the boulevard. If I intended to have a conversation at this juncture I would need to scream into a bullhorn in order to make myself heard.

An outdoor café farther along the walkway has posted a sign that reads "Breakfast and Margaritas." This juxtaposition might seem peculiar to someone who has just arrived, but it is not extraordinary for this wild place. Pancakes and a shot of Johnny Walker is probably no more peculiar here than bacon and eggs. Breakfast and margaritas. Lunch and margaritas. Whatever you are munching on and margaritas.

The sidewalk is littered with cards that feature photographs of provocative women who are referred to on these mini-advertisements as "escorts." The sidewalk is also littered with the people who are distributing the cards. As many as twenty such hawkers crowd any two-block stretch. Typically they're located in clusters, and each has a deck of these photos. As you approach the cluster, the shills snap the cards to gain your attention before extending a photo, hoping you will take one and reduce the stash they are required to give away.

All along the Strip are March Madness bettors, walking from one sports book to another, holding line sheets in front of their faces as they negotiate the sidewalks. Close to the Venetian I find myself behind two such fellows. They are from Tucson, they tell me. When I ask them who they like, they inform me contrapuntally, without glancing backward, that Arizona is a lock to win their upcoming game on Friday and will easily cover the 2½-point spread. They are walking at a pretty good clip and are speaking with something approaching arrogance—as if they are talking to a dullard.

"Who do you like?" I ask.

"Arizona," says A.

"Arizona," confirms B.

"In the bank," says A.

"Count it," says B with a snort.

"In the bank," repeats A.

"Count it," repeats B.

I interrupt the commentary. "You like Arizona, eh?"

"Yes, we like Arizona, eh," says A.

"Purdue has no shot. None," says B.

I find their certainty both comical and irksome. I decide to be contrary and shout over their shoulders. "I heard that Purdue will not only beat the spread, but will win on the money line."

This slows A and B down a beat. They look at each other. B turns around and stares at me as if I am not only a fool, but rude to doubt their wisdom.

"Arizona wins and covers," he sneers.

These fellows, it turns out, are as wrong as they are certain. This malady infects a large portion of the betting population and is, I imagine, a source of great joy among gaming entrepreneurs. On Friday, not only does Arizona not cover the spread, they lose the game to Purdue.

Shouda Looked at My Ticket

The Venetian looks like a hotel in, well, Venice, and enough is conventional about the facility to make you forget that you are in Las Vegas. The hotel has a very elegant lobby, beautiful gift shops, families with young children, and even canals outside with gondolas and serenading gondoliers.

But the sports book is something else. There must be a thousand wild men in this jumping room late Thursday afternoon on this first day of March Madness. Unlike Bally's, the Paris, and the Imperial Palace, the Venetian sports book does not have the feel or look of an auditorium. It is essentially a huge space in a section of the casino that is dedicated to sports wagering. Many of the seats in the book are comfortable easy chairs. The book contains about thirty rows of these chairs with as many as forty chairs in each row.

The rectangular bar at the back of the room doubles as a demarcation line separating the rest of the casino from the sports book. It has twenty barstools on each of its longer sides. Bar patrons on the side closer to the sports book can swivel 180 degrees and, like everyone else in the book, view any one of the four enormous screens that are embedded in the front wall. Smaller televisions below the huge four carry other events. Flanking the large screens is an electronic scoreboard that reports the scores and lines for all contests on which there is action. Bar patrons on the far side can watch the games on any one of several televisions above the bar. No matter where you sit in the Venetian sports book you have a good viewing angle of any of several sporting events.

An aisle bisects the rows of easy chairs. The betting queue forms in the aisle, and on this Thursday the line of bettors extends nearly to the bar. In the three hours I watch games, the size of the line ebbs during the middle of contests, but for nearly the entire period dozens of beery men wait on this queue either to make a bet or collect on a winning wager.

The place is absolutely jammed. It is so crowded that groups of bettors appear to have camped out in open spaces in the front of the book, not sitting in chairs but sprawled on the rug, having commandeered the area like squatters. A thick and continuous cluster of men lean against the wall to the far left of the book. They chatter with their cronies about the wisdom of this pick or that, holding and pointing to their betting sheets and slips. So many men line this wall that any gap between the wall and the first sets of chairs is extraordinarily narrow. This creates difficulty for waitresses attempting to deliver beverages and makes the route to the betting sheets in the front of the book impossible to navigate without bumps and jostles. The Venetian is just packed and rocking.

The beer is free at the Venetian as long as you can produce a betting ticket indicating that you have placed a wager. Almost every soul in this enormous sports book has enough tickets to ruin his liver. Nearly naked waitresses take orders and bring the beer to the bettors and receive a tip for their efforts. Usually the tip is $1 per drink, so a beer that typically costs $5 sets the patron back a single dollar. The Venetian is donating bottles of beer that may cost thirty cents a piece from a wholesaler.

This is a win-win-win situation. It's a win for the waitresses, who are making $50 to $75 every fifteen minutes as they make their rounds. It's a huge win for the casino. The return on their "free" beer is thousands of dollars from amateur bettors who cannot wait to toss away hundreds of dollars a pop on "can't miss" propositions. And it's a win for the bettors, who think they are getting a free beer and moreover, regardless of winning or losing, seem to be having the time of their lives.

I can't find a single seat in the facility so I stand with my back to a corner of the bar overlooking the throng of well-watered patrons. Next to me is a man in his forties who works for Caterpillar, as I soon learn. He is reserved initially but eventually I engage him. Dressed in relatively formal attire, he is here for a convention. He is dour and appears to be observing the games almost disdainfully. He comments that the scene is not for him; he doesn't drink or gamble, and while he's a Hoosier through and through and has managed to find the sports book to cheer on Indiana, he doesn't care for the sordid nature of Las Vegas. Shortly after he makes this comment, he nearly snaps his head off checking out a cocktail waitress.

We are standing very close to where the waitresses fill their trays with drinks in response to the insatiable demand of the bettors. A space in front of us separates the bar area from the seated audience. Every few minutes a parade of waitresses pass by hauling sustenance. On the other side of me, away from the Caterpillar employee, a bettor quips, "Ought to give her a buck just for walking through."

When he returns his focus, the Caterpillar employee tells me about how good Indiana is and identifies every one of the players. Most, but not all, of the bettors are not concerned with the names of individual players, except as such familiarity helps them handicap the games. If they know a particular center is an asset and can make a difference in terms of points or rebounds, they may be able to identify him. Once the game is on, however, whether it is Joe or Shmo who makes a shot is irrelevant. If the ball goes in, it is either good or bad for betting, regardless of who tosses it in. The time for marveling at an individual's prowess is not when you need your team to cover the spread.

After a spell I get tired of standing next to the bar. Because of the constant traffic in the aisle it is difficult to get a consistent view of the games. I scout the rows of chairs for an empty space and am fortunate to find an excellent spot in the third row. Usually, to get a seat in this section one has to arrive with the roosters. After I settle in I discover that the people next to me have done just that. They stumbled into their seats at 4:45 a.m.

My immediate neighbor is a fifty-eight-year-old retired executive who has lived all over the world. With his brother and a group of three other 1972 University of Arkansas alums he has come to Las Vegas this year for the twenty-second consecutive time. My neighbor, in a drawl worthy of any Razorback despite his globetrotting, tells me that he missed one year because he had been invited to a high-stakes poker championship. In the two hours I am seated with him and his cronies, none in their party consume anything harder than iced tea. These folks are anomalies among the beer guzzling masses. For several minutes my neighbor recounts, sadly, the heartbreak that was the last minutes of the 1971 Arkansas–Texas Cotton Bowl.

My new friend from Arkansas becomes a victim, almost comically, of a regular phenomenon that can affect the unsophisticated bettor. The sheets that post the spreads and other data for the games are not a guarantee of the spreads or odds bettors will receive when they get to the window. The line fluctuates depending on how much money is placed on one team or the other. Most pundits, though not all, suggest that the spread for the game varies in order to ensure that money is equally wagered on both sides of the game. Consequently, when Central Connecticut State is listed as receiving 22½ points in its match with Ohio State the idea is that half of the money will be placed on Ohio State and half on Central Connecticut. However, if the opening spread of 22½ points seems very attractive to bettors wagering on Central Connecticut—and consequently, more bets are placed on them—the casino will reduce the spread so that more money will be placed on Ohio State.

This is precisely what occurred to my friend from Arkansas when he took Central Connecticut State and the 22½ points— or so he told me.

"Here's my thinkin'. Central Connecticut plays excellent defense. Right? Ohio State is outstandin', but can they really score twenty-two and a half points more than a team that takes its sweet slow-as-molasses time every single time they go to take a shot?

"I did not think so. But apparently," he chuckles and points at me, "apparently, so did many others who bet on the game, because when I checked my ticket I noticed something I shouda observed when I was issued the slip initially. Instead of twenty-two and a half points I was gettin' twenty." My friend from Arkansas again laughs at himself and the incident.

"All right. So here's what happens. Score's seventy-eight–fifty-seven. Only seconds left and Central Connecticut has a fast break. Some kid from Connecticut pulls up for a three and it is a brick. Kid had a three on two break, but he shoots the three.

"My hunch," continues Arkansas, "is that if he drives for the two the Buckeyes say 'Go to town,' but instead the kid goes for the three. And there I am holding a ticket getting twenty points, not twenty-two and a half, in a game that ends seventy-eight–fifty-seven. Kid drives to the bucket, game ends seventy-eight–fifty-nine and I'm a winner. Game ends seventy-eight–fifty-seven, though, and I'm a loser."

Arkansas shakes his head amused. "Fact is. Shouda looked at my ticket." He waves his hand. "No big deal," he says. "This whole thing is great fun."

Etiquette

My bets are in for the last contests of the day. On the advice of a stranger I met this morning at Bally's, whom I suspect is now well on his way to drunken oblivion, I am taking the 27 points and going with Eastern Kentucky in its game against North Carolina. The stranger had opined that "four touchdowns" were too many points for North Carolina to sacrifice. Why not accept the counsel from an unknown twenty-one-year old who was on his second beer before 9 a.m.? My second bet is similarly founded on the advice of a stranger, albeit in this case a sober one. I decide to respect the Caterpillar man's insights and have wagered on Indiana conceding 1½ points to Gonzaga. According to another pundit I overheard several hours ago, Gonzaga tends to disappoint in the tournament. Finally, I have bet on Xavier against Brigham Young University, conceding 2½ points even though the spread was listed as 2 on the betting sheet. In addition to these individual wagers, I'm employing the "system" advanced by the delinquent Salisbury State University student. I have the three single bets and a parlay that combines all three games. I have no real sense that these bets are wise, but after almost an entire day of this it seems to me that few others in this town have this sense either.

A verbal brawl is taking place nearby. Two men standing in the aisle to my right are barking at hats-backward college students seated in the row right behind me and the fellows from Arkansas. The men in the aisle look to be nearly fifty and are dressed unconventionally for a sports book in white suits with dark shirts, as if they are extras in an old *Miami Vice* episode. Judging from their accent they both speak English as a second language, but they are quite vociferous in their complaint that the college students have taken their seats. They claim that they arrived at the Venetian at 4 in the morning to secure their spots and the college kids are poachers.

The students are anything but rude when they explain their position. They say they waited thirty minutes staring at the vacant seats. They argue that arriving at 4 a.m. does not allow you to leave for an hour, go elsewhere, and retain the seats when you return. The suited men are adamant and keep using the word "etiquette." The casino etiquette, they say, is to honor the person who arrived early.

"Not all day," replies the spokesperson for the students, a young man whose T-shirt reads, "I Got Bent in Dent. First Annual Testicle Festival."

One of the suits pleads his case profanely. He speaks to not only the students, but extends his plea to all of us in the vicinity, who are in fact tiring of the distraction. He holds his arms out and presents his crude argument as if speaking to a jury.

"Sometimes you have to take a shit," says the suit in a voice that is far too loud given the coarse language.

To this line of reasoning, someone behind the quarrel whose sight line has been obscured offers the following sober and mature suggestion:

"Why don't you fucking guys sit the fuck down and shut the fuck up."

The students maintain their equanimity despite the suits' appeals and the request from the rear. "Look, we waited thirty minutes," says a young man calmly.

The suits are getting hot, as are the more well-watered spec-

tators who are having trouble concentrating on the games because of the distraction. The students do not budge and seem
to be the victors in this battle. However, the older men return
with security guards who ask the college students to relinquish
their seats. My take is that some money has been exchanged. It
does not make sense that the security guards would make a case
for one party over another in a matter of apparently legitimate
if contrasting claims. There seems to be some weight behind
the security guards' requests, or so the students believe. One kid
says to the other, "C'mon Chuck. It's not worth it." Reluctantly
the students stand up and leave. The suits reclaim the spots.

I turn around as they get settled in their seats. As if he believes
that I am an apologist for the students, one of the gentlemen
repeats his logic to me. "It's etiquette. Sometimes you have to
take a shit." Then he shrugs his shoulders as if to say, "Isn't that
obvious? Isn't that logical?"

•••

It looks like Eastern Kentucky is going to be a winning bet. The
inebriate who argued for betting on them—accepting the four
touchdowns—had some wisdom. North Carolina is victorious
but only by three touchdowns. Also, the Caterpillar man has
given me a good tip, as Indiana clobbers Gonzaga. Apparently
Gonzaga always does disappoint. However, the Xavier game is
painfully close, and it appears as if it will break my parlay. I am
sweating out the last seconds of the game when my friend from
Arkansas leans over and asks what initially at least seems to be a
bizarre question.

"How much you laying?" he says.

It sounds so odd and I don't quite get it.

"What?" I respond.

"You laying two?"

I understand the inquiry the second time. In the parlance of the bettor you lay points if you bet the favorite, so he wanted to know how much I was conceding. I knew that, but with this exchange I discover that I am not yet fluent in the jargon of the sports book.

"I'm laying two and a half," I say in response, but it sounds funny to me as it comes out of my mouth.

He nods soberly.

So, I am laying two and a half.

It looks like I am going to win this bet and win another parlay. Xavier is winning 79–75 with only seconds to go. Since I am laying 2½ I am therefore ahead by 1½ points. However, the ball is loose near the Brigham Young basket. Both teams scramble for the ball. No matter who retrieves it, the actual game is over. Since basketball doesn't have a 4-point goal and only 3 seconds are remaining, even if BYU were to collect the ball and score— even a miraculous 3-point heave—Xavier would win the contest. But winning the contest may not be good enough for me because I am laying 2½.

BYU wins the scrum and retrieves the ball with only 1 second to play. They hoist a shot. It goes in. Instead of the final being 79–75, it is 79–77. I have laid half a point too much.

The collective groan in the Venetian collides with a collective shout of glee as one contingent is a loser and another a winner on the basis of a meaningless last-second field goal.

"How much did you lay again?" asks the Razorback.

I tell him.

"Ooohhh," he says. "Sorry," he chuckles. "Sorta like my Central Connecticut disaster . . ."

And so to compound my loss, I'm obliged to listen to the Razorback relay once again how Central Connecticut could have covered the 20-point spread earlier in the day by just "drivin' to the bucket" instead of "takin' that gosh darn three."

•••

It's almost ten o'clock Pacific time. It has been a long day since the man from Texas A&M bounded out of the elevator on his way to the Imperial Palace sports book and a fellow in the Paris bar marked the beginning of March Madness by saying "Gentle-men, start your engines." I've watched sixteen basketball games today, and I don't think I want to count how many beers I have consumed.

I must be beginning to behave like a regular because on the way back to my room at the Imperial Palace I stop at the sports book and pick up the betting sheets for Friday. It is late. There are no games on the screens. I look around the auditorium.

I am not alone. Scattered throughout the amphitheater are groups of bettors trying to predict tomorrow.

You Got a Lock?

A hundred people must be in line to place a bet at Bally's on Friday morning at 8, just hours after many of these same people have lost their shirts. Like yesterday, the tables are jammed with mostly young men in T-shirts and baseball caps turned backward jawing about Georgia Tech and Nevada and Oregon and any one or all of the thirty-two teams who have yet to begin play. Where seats are vacant the chairs have been pushed forward, sending a "No Trespassing" message.

Buckets of beers already sit on the tables. Men who, at home, would never consider indulging before noon eased into a different zone yesterday, so today at 8 seems like a suitable time to start knocking them back. To capitalize on the fondness for alcohol in this environment, Bally's has advertised a special: five bottles of beer for $20. The beers are served jammed in a plastic bucket filled with ice. This price has almost doubled in just one year: in 2006 the special was four beers for $10. Inflation does not seem to be affecting consumption. What's a few dollars more for a brew when you are ready to relinquish $100 to see if a school in Corpus Christi can cover a 13-point spread? Never mind that Corpus Christi could be on the moon as far as you are concerned—you have $100 riding on whether this basketball team can play good D and hit the 3. Let the beer flow.

Bally's, as opposed to some other sports books such as the Venetian, does not freely provide drinks to its customers. The decisions of managers in this regard can seem capricious. At the Imperial Palace, for example, if you sit in one room beverages are complimentary. If you sit in another, they are not. Typically the rationale is based on the game or sport on which patrons are wagering. Managers do not want to encourage horse bettors, for example, to leave their seats, as multiple races at several tracks often occur concurrently during the course of the day. In the time it takes to purchase a drink, the $6 a customer spends on the beverage can deprive a casino of $60 that might have been wagered during the same interval, hoping that a trotter in Hialeah can finish in the money. Basketball bettors, on the other hand, place bets at the beginning, and perhaps at the half, of two-hour contests. A patron who ambles to the bar to replenish a drink during the second half of a basketball game is not likely to reduce the handle. Nevertheless, it can seem strange to walk a few steps and purchase a beer for $6, and walk a few steps more and find that you can get one for free.

On the tables next to the buckets of beers are the omnipresent betting sheets and, of course, the huddled bettors. This morning Memphis is an 18-point favorite in its matchup with North Texas. This I consider—in my desire to master and employ the idiom of the casino—to be a lot of lumber to lay down. Georgia Tech is only giving up 1½ to the University of Nevada at Las Vegas. The best bet, I know, is Virginia laying only 7½ points to the University of Albany. However, I cannot bring myself to bet against my alma mater. I know I would be tossing $20 into the wind wagering that Albany will finish within a dozen of Virginia, let alone 7½, but an emotional tug precludes anything other than a donation to some casino's hold.

I am dressed for the Albany game like a fevered alumnus, wearing an Albany Great Dane shirt, cap, and a pair of Great Dane socks. In an interval of fifteen minutes three bettors with pencils in their ears notice my attire and stop by to ask me if Albany can cover. Reluctantly, I tell them what I believe. They nod, say thank you, and as likely as not, bet on whomever that they had intended to wager on before they made my brief acquaintance.

Someone else I have not met previously suddenly confronts me. This backward-capped fellow wearing an outrageously obscene T-shirt stares at me eyeball to eyeball, then grimly and with a sense of urgency asks a question that could only make sense in a hardware store.

"You got a lock?"

I do have a lock, but I am reluctant to criticize the Great Danes further. Moreover, my performance yesterday, except for a few atypical successes, makes me reluctant to tell anyone I have a lock on anything. So, instead of telling him that I have a lock, I tell him that judging by yesterday's performance I have no locks and consider suggesting that no one among the hundreds swirling around has one either.

•••

I walk across the street to the Flamingo because I'm not sure if I will make it down the ramp at Bally's in time to get my bets in. Unfortunately, the line is also long at the Flamingo. One person appears to be taking inordinate time at the window, incurring the wrath of the many others standing behind him.

Conversation on the queue includes musings on the games and sharing assorted tips. It seems odd that many bettors will get in a line that leads to a cashier with whom they will deposit hundreds of dollars on wagers *before* determining where their money will be placed. Why would customers yell for a line to move rapidly if they're unsure of what they intend to purchase? I consider this phenomenon as I too wait on the line, not quite sure of where I will be placing my wager. It strikes me that most of the amateurs standing here—including myself—are essentially waiting to buy a ticket for a ride as opposed to making a wager on one team or another. The bettors may like North Texas with the points more than Memphis without them, but, hypothetically, if for some reason customers were told when they reached the cashier that all the tickets for North Texas were gone, the people on this queue would probably bet on Memphis just to be able to enjoy the thrill of the roller coaster.

Directly in front of me in the queue are three buddies from James Madison University, a Virginia state school located in Harrisonburg. I overhear their chatter. One of them—whom the others refer to as Buster—says that North Texas has great athletes according to a fellow he met at a blackjack table the night before. Buster suggests to his friends that they place a $100 bet on North Texas because of this wisdom from someone he happened to sit adjacent to while they were both squandering their savings playing blackjack. One of the other Harrisonburg friends leaves as we wait on this interminable line, then returns with beers for his crew. Just like yesterday at the Paris, these fellows hoist their brews and with amusement make the same toast I'd heard twenty-four hours before: "Top of the morning!" They begin knocking back their Coronas at 8:45.

Behind me is an ironworker from Chicago. He tells me that he lost four grand on Duke losing to Virginia Commonwealth yesterday. I cannot believe that someone lost $4,000 in one day betting on these games. The expression on my face must reflect my disbelief, because Mike from Chicago explains in more detail.

"I didn't actually lose four grand. It's that I should have won four grand which I lost because fucking Duke could not beat vcu." He proceeds to tell me about this "can't miss" parlay he had that only required Duke to defeat vcu.

"vcu? Against Duke? I mean, I'm talking the money line here, not the spread. Duke could not even beat vcu. Cost me four fucking thousand dollars."

Mike from Chicago, now four fucking thousand dollars short, continues to expound. He tells me that he travels the entire country working on one construction project or another, but he always comes to Las Vegas for March Madness.

"I tell the wife that I'm going out with three grand and I intend to make four grand."

"How is it going this year?" I inquire more to be wise than to get a straight answer.

He waves a paw and snorts. "Forgetaboutit. Fucking Duke," he says. "But I love Georgia Tech and Notre Dame today."

As we continue to converse I begin to wonder if his wife doesn't figure it is worth the three grand just to get this guy out of the house for four days. Mike explains that he only bets the money line on the parlays because that is where you can make the cash. This information and betting strategy is at odds, of course, with the news that he has not yet won anything. Oblivious to this irony, Mike continues to explain the merits of money line betting.

"You're pissing your dough away otherwise," says a man who is $4,000 in the hole by his own accounting.

• • •

I can't get the 9:15 bet in on time at the Flamingo, and it's a blessing since I would have gone emotionally with Albany. Still, it's frustrating not to be able to place the wager. The Harrison-burg trio is furious because they are unsure now if they will get the money down on the North Texas game, which is scheduled to start only a few minutes after the Albany–Virginia tip-off. The Harrisonburg three know the North Texas game is a lock on the basis of the wisdom spewed about North Texas from someone at a blackjack table.

The fellow at the front of the window seems to be asking many questions. "Get the fuck from the window!" screams Bust-er. He takes a swig from his beer and shakes his head. "Oh, what the hell," he says, "this is better than 'Contemporary Political Theory' with Robinson." This gets a round of laughter from his James Madison University pals. It is time for another toast.

"Here's to the poor bastards now sitting in 'Contemporary Political Theory,'" says Buster.

The boys from Harrisonburg drink up.

The Notebook

The Flamingo sports book has a very small seating area for spec-tators. Not only is it undersized, but because it is undersized it lacks the energy and zaniness of the other casinos. In pursuit of zany and knowing very well where I can find it, I cross back over Flamingo Road to watch the Albany game in Bally's.

It is no surprise that Bally's is as crowded as it was when I left to attempt to place my bets at the Flamingo. However, I do no-tice what seems to be a single seat at one of the long tables that have been set up in the bar area for this weekend. At this table several young men cluster around someone else seated at the table, looking over his shoulder and jabbering about something. Because they're bunched together I can't quite determine how many of them there are, and so I'm not sure whether the open seat is indeed available. I make my way to the group and ask about the seat. They very politely tell me that the seat is mine, so I grab it. They then return to their confab, examining whatever it is that has been placed in front of their seated companion.

I discover that the young men are discussing upcoming wagers as they review a notebook compiled by one of their numbers that analyzes player and team statistics. After a spell the discussion seems to be over and the five take their seats and prepare to watch the games. I ask if I can take a look at what they have been studying.

The notebook is like none other I have ever seen. It is unusually detailed and extremely well organized. The author has divided the contents into several parts and has placed dividers in the book to separate one section from another. Information related to each region in the tournament has its own part in the book. The initial divider in the notebook has a label that reads "South Regional." On the first page is a list of all the teams playing in the south regional; the next page is headed with the words "Ohio State," the 1 seed in the South Regional. On the Ohio State page I find the team's 2006–2007 overall record, the record in away games, the record in home games, NCAA history, how or why they were invited to the tournament, the player roster, and the class year of players who play more than ten minutes a game. At the bottom of the page is a paragraph that appears to be written by the compiler of this encyclopedia. The paragraph summarizes the data on the page and assesses Ohio State's chances for success in the tournament. The next page in the section is headed with the word "Memphis." And for the Memphis Tigers—the 2 seed in the South—the same categories of information appear as on the Ohio State page. This information set is provided for each of the remaining teams in the tournament.

The notebook contains over a hundred pages. After the breakdowns for all four regions and each of the teams comes a section on first-round matchups and predicted second-round matches. The book has an appendix with various items such as box scores, prior tournament bracket sheets, and experts' predictions. It is a startlingly thorough document. I ask the author if he is a college student, and he confirms that he attends a school in Grand Rapids, Michigan. I wonder if for any of his classes he has ever put together a manuscript as impressive.

I ask if the book helps with his handicapping. He shrugs and sheepishly tells me that he is down $200 from yesterday. He adds quickly, however, that the group has a bundle on Albany this morning, and according to the data compiled he feels good about the chances of recouping yesterday's losses in short time.

By halftime it is clear that Albany will be trounced regardless of the psychological energy generated by my wearing Great Dane apparel or the wisdom contained in the notebook on our table. A player from Virginia named J. R. Reynolds is shooting like Michael Jordan, connecting on his first seven shots including four 3-pointers. Virginia is playing as if it had become annoyed listening to how this Albany team from the inferior America East was going to beat players from the Atlantic Coast Conference. Virginia also seems to have learned a lesson from the University of Connecticut's narrow escape the previous year. Albany is behind by 20 points at the half, and the prospects for a comeback are not very good.

During the intermission the young man from Grand Rapids reviews the information in his notebook. He shakes his head, bewildered, as if what he is seeing on the screen just does not make sense given his comprehensive analysis. He is bewildered throughout the second half as well because Virginia covers the 7½ and then some. They are victorious in the contest by nearly 30 points.

Meanwhile Memphis is defeating North Texas but not sufficiently to overcome the 18-point spread. The outcome makes the fellow at the blackjack table appear to be a sage, and the Harrisonburg three, wherever they may be, are likely winners. To the delight of those rooting for the home team, the University of Nevada at Las Vegas is holding its own against Georgia Tech and may not just cover the spread, but may win the game outright. At least one person in the sports book is not rooting for the home team. At what seems like regular intervals, this fellow repeatedly and less-than-creatively curses Georgia Tech because, apparently, he is upset at the team's inability to help him win a wager.

•••

I leave the long table at the bar to go to the amphitheater while the Grand Rapids kids are still shaking their heads at how their notebook has deceived them. I find myself standing in the back of the auditorium next to two young men from the Bronx. We chat about how difficult it is to find seats in Bally's. One of the buddies elbows his friend and points to four vacant chairs in a prime location. We go to scout them out and see that the chairs have a sign on them that reads "Reserved for Cold Pizza." *Cold Pizza* is an ESPN2 program, and apparently representatives have been given these reserved seats. It is very common in a sports book to find "open" seats that have been reserved for a media representative. It is also not uncommon for these seats to remain vacant for extended periods of time. The Bronx fellows look at me, and I at them, and wordlessly we grab the empty seats. Once seated, we discuss the heist and conclude that if *Cold Pizza* representatives arrive we will move. I, for one, am aware of the etiquette, having been a witness to the fracas with the suits yesterday. However, no one from *Cold Pizza* ever arrives. We sit in the VIP seats for an hour's worth of games.

One of the Bronx guys, Greg, has a cigar. As he is considering future wagers, he sniffs the cigar, occasionally puts it in his mouth, places it on top of a small paper plate in front of him, but never lights up. Wade, his companion, comments that he thinks they should go with Tennessee because Bruce Pearl is a New Yorker and unequivocally a very smart coach. I find Wade's analysis amusing, since just yesterday I overheard someone say he was going to bet against Tennessee and would put a wad on Long Beach State. He asserted just as unequivocally that "Bruce Pearl knows shit."

And there you have it, two sides to every story. This is what makes the sports book the sports book. I think to tell Greg and Wade what I'd heard about Bruce Pearl yesterday but decide to pass. I'm not sure anyone in Bally's knows whether Bruce Pearl is a "very smart coach" or "knows shit."

Greg takes the cigar out of his mouth and says, "Okay, let's lay the lumber on Tennessee." He gets up to go on line to place the bet. A group of raucous, rowdy Notre Dame fans are seated around us. Shortly, Notre Dame will be tipping off against Winthrop, a school from South Carolina.

"Go Irish!" one of them shouts every few seconds or so, like an old-time record that is skipping. He must say "Go Irish!" ten times in five minutes. This causes Greg to shake his head:

"Go Irish," he mimics, "go where? Guarantee that Winthrop will cover."

You Just Don't Know

At the half of the 11:30 games I leave Wade and Greg, walk out of Bally's, cross Flamingo Road, and go through the Flamingo Hotel, down the Strip, into the Imperial Palace, and up to the ballroom. Walking the half mile or so, I count twenty-five people around me who are studying betting sheets, all looking as if they are trying to make sense out of a map that will lead them to a buried treasure.

As Mike Fay told me, a big Wisconsin following has gathered at the Imperial Palace. In addition, a pack of Notre Dame fans have seized a set of tables. The Notre Dame rooters are not happy. Four-point underdog Winthrop is ahead of Notre Dame throughout the game and has as large as a 20-point advantage before blowing the lead entirely late in the second half. The comeback excited the Notre Dame rooters, but Winthrop responded to the run and eventually wins by 10 points. I am sure Greg and Wade from the Bronx are happy, but the leprechauns look sad in the Imperial Palace ballroom.

I've been watching this game unfold sitting next to a fellow named Wally from New Jersey. He's been anxious throughout the second half, but having bet on Winthrop, is eventually delighted by the win. Every so often throughout the game, he slaps the table, looks at me, chuckles, and raises his eyebrows. When it's over he makes a speech, sounding as if he knew the game was in the bag all the way.

"I knew this was a lock," he begins. "Winthrop was underrated all year. Notre Dame plays in the Big East so everyone thinks, 'Oh boy, they play in the Big East.' I knew Winthrop would handle them. Let me tell you something, Al. They're gonna win on Sunday."

"You think so?"

"Oh. Yeah." Then he nods repeatedly and purses his lips. "I'm going to bet big on them on Sunday."

The Winthrop victory proved to be valuable to the casinos and costly to Wally. It was the kind of tease that the sports books love. Later in the afternoon Oregon, a 9-point favorite, barely beat its opponent, Miami of Ohio. Oregon would play Winthrop on Sunday. The result of the Winthrop win and the Oregon narrow escape makes amateur bettors like Wally and me think that Winthrop will do well against Oregon on Sunday. Anyone who succumbed to such a notion would, in fact, be a big loser on

Sunday, when Oregon pummeled Winthrop by 14, easily over-coming the illogically low 3½-point spread.

I bumped into Wally late on Sunday, and he wailed that he had bet Winthrop not only with the spread but also on the money line and as part of a parlay. He makes another speech.

"Fucking Winthrop," he begins. "Fucking Winthrop," he continues. "Did they lay an egg or what? They play great against Notre Dame, raise up my hopes and then they lay an egg. You know what it shows, don't you?"

"What does it show?" I ask him.

"You just don't know."

"You just don't know?"

"It just goes to show you," Wally says and takes a very deep breath, "you just don't know."

●●●

The Notre Dame fans are not the only ones sulking. The Wisconsin faithful are apprehensive because the Badgers need to beat the University of Texas at Corpus Christi by 13, and they lead by only 10 with 1:54 to play.

Wisconsin has the ball and is content—without any consideration for those who have bet on them—to run out the clock. Corpus Christi is determined—without any consideration for those who have bet on them—to foul and force Wisconsin to make foul shots. After a foul, a Texas bettor wails from somewhere in the ballroom, "What are you doing?"

Neither team's bettors are happy when the game ends. The final is 76–63. With the 13-point spread, this game, in the jargon of the casino, is a push. Nobody wins. The Wisconsin fans are moping because they figure they certainly should have been able to trounce a pissant school like Corpus Christi. The Texas fans are upset because if the team had given up when they were down by 10 and not fouled, their wagers on Texas would have been successful.

Greg and Wade, my fellow seat poachers at Bally's, apparently had the goods on Bruce Pearl, their kinsman from New York. Tennessee obliterates Long Beach State by 35, the margin five times as much as the boys from the Bronx needed to win their money from the casino. Bruce Pearl knew some shit after all.

Come on Mikey, Sit Down

Sometime after the 2006 March Madness, the Imperial Palace renovated its sports book betting area to make it more spacious and comfortable for those queuing up on the lines. In the past the attendants who took the bets stood behind a counter in a small room that would become crammed, noisy, and occasionally malodorous during peak periods. Patrons waiting to wager would be bunched uncomfortably because the lines were constrained by a rear wall. To address the problem, the counters have been moved from the small room to the front of the adjacent large amphitheater. Now, eighty bettors or more can stand unconstrained in the line.

Consequently, this year, the Imperial Palace has yet a third place for viewing the games. The vacated space that had been the betting area has been transformed into a relatively intimate room for spectators who may sit around small tables that have been placed directly in view of large television sets. This is an excellent arrangement for patrons who are wagering on or interested in a single game. If you want to see several contests at the same time, this third area is not a good spot, since from any one table it's difficult to see the other television screens.

I spend some time in this undersized space on Friday afternoon. One of the small round tables has seven bettors wedged

shoulder to shoulder around it. Everyone at this table is rooting for Illinois in its game against Virginia Tech. With only 17
seconds left, Illinois, a 3-point underdog, is losing by 2, 54–52.
If this score holds up, anyone who wagered on Illinois and had
received the 3 points would be victorious by a single point,
55–54.

An Illinois player rebounds a missed Virginia Tech free throw
and calls a time-out. During the recess one would assume that
Illinois' coach would be calling a play that could result in a high-
percentage shot that might tie or win the game. However, after
the time-out an Illinois player gathers the in-bounded pass and,
without any apparent plan whatsoever, chucks up an ill-advised
3-point shot in what appears to be a senseless attempt to win the
game. The shot misses, but with 3 seconds remaining the same
player who took the shot secures the rebound and is fouled.

A sober-looking man who looks like he might teach algebra
somewhere in rural Illinois bolts up and screams like crazy. He
is truly furious.

"That's the play you draw up?! That's the goddamn play you
draw up?" Then this outraged fanatic turns to his friends at the
table, opens his hands, and asks despairingly, "That's the goddamn play they draw up?"

"Sit down, Mikey. Come on. Sit down," says one of his friends.

As he slumps back into his chair, Mikey mutters the same words
again, this time as more of a resigned wheeze than an exclamation
or inquiry. "That's the goddamn play they draw up," he says as he
nods his head up and down quickly. The man is still steamed.

All is not lost for Illinois. Because of the foul, the Illinois player who rebounded the ball, Brian Randle, has been awarded one
and one. "One and one" in basketball jargon means that a fouled
player is given an opportunity to take a single free throw and will
be granted a second if the first attempt is good.

Ironically, an Illinois bettor will win this game if Randle misses the first foul shot. If he makes the first one and misses the
second the Illinois bettor will also win the bet. However, if Randle makes both shots the game will be tied, and the contest will
likely go into overtime. Then anything could occur to affect the
success of the wager. Consequently, an Illinois fan wants both
shots to go through while an Illinois bettor hopes for a miss.

The people huddled around the table seem to be much less
like bettors and much more like fans. When Brian Randle reaches the foul line, seven solemn don't-mess-with-me forty-some-
thing-year-old men—all top to bottom festooned with Illinois
paraphernalia—are locked on the screen.

Brian Randle misses the first shot.

When the foul shot clanks away, Mikey takes a pencil, throws
it at the television as hard as he can, and directs the following
comment to the Illinois basketball player who has missed a free
throw: "You miserable goddamn scumbag sonofabitch."

Under ordinary circumstances I might like to interview Mikey
for my book, but I do not want to get close to this lunatic.

Illinois bettors were winners after Brian Randle's miss. Mikey
and his cohorts were not betting men, at least on this game.
They were fans.

Two Hot Dogs

On March 7, 2007, two weeks before my encounter with Mikey,
I found myself backstage at Madison Square Garden. I was seated at a table in a makeshift cafeteria set up directly behind press
row, underneath the stands, beyond guarded doors. I was attending the first round of the Big East basketball tournament as a
member of the press corps.

In the fall of 2006 I had contacted the sports information directors of several athletic conferences and requested a media

credential for specific games during the season. I thought I might obtain an interesting perspective on college basketball by sitting at press row. I was not quite sure what I might find, but I thought I might observe something different from what I would see in the stands and it could be a help as I worked on this book.

By March 7 I had attended several games as a member of the fourth estate. Most recently I had been at the first round of the America East tournament, flown to Richmond for the final two rounds of the Colonial Athletic Association tournament, and flown back to New York for the Big East. It had been quite a ride.

Now, on March 7—this first day of the Big East tournament—I am armed with my media credentials beneath the seats at Madison Square Garden. Big East Conference officials have appropriated this backstage space for, literally, their behind-the-scenes operation. The huge area—easily the size of a football field—has been separated into three sections. On one side is a podium and a dozen rows of chairs reserved for postgame interviews with coaches and players. By this point in my media meanderings I have seen similar arrangements many times. The Big East, a very prestigious conference, has more seats for its postgame press conferences than the other arenas where I have been, but whether it has been in Binghamton or Boston or Richmond, the drill is always the same. After a game, reporters gather in an area like this and wait. First they wait for a few players and the head coach of the victorious team to arrive, make a statement, and take questions. Then they wait for representative players and the head coach of the losing team to arrive, make a statement, and field questions.

At every single postgame media session like this, the statements and responses to questions are almost exactly the same. The winning coaches and players talk about how it had been a team win. Everyone contributed. They played the good D, played to their potential, and were very satisfied with the outcome. They praise the opponents magnanimously. Then the coaches and players take questions and answer them so predictably that after attending a few of these sessions I am nearly positive that I know what the responses will be to nearly all of the questions. The dance of the losing players and head coach is similar except these individuals bemoan not playing the good D, not playing up to their potential, not being satisfied with the outcome, and so on.

Next to the press conference space is the largest of the three sections. In this area dozens of long tables have been placed for journalists from all over the country to set up their laptops and write game reports. These tables are packed. Despite the hundreds of chairs very few are vacant. This middle area is a hectic center of activity: computer experts assist journalists, media assistants shuttle from the room out to the arena and then bolt back again, journalists type frantically to meet deadlines, reporters scan the crowd trying to locate colleagues, sportscasters talk on their cell phones. The joint is jumping.

The space on the other side of the middle section has been converted into a cafeteria. The cafeteria entrance is guarded by a Garden employee who checks media passes to ensure that no interloper can access the catered fare.

And it is here at the cafeteria where I sit talking to a fellow named Roger from Syracuse who is the chief executive officer of a company employed by the Big East and other conferences. Just moments ago, at the press conference after the Syracuse–Connecticut game, I heard the predictable drivel from the participants, then passed the frenzied correspondents at the long tables.

Our conversation is interesting and entertaining. I discover that this young man, who is no more than thirty-five years old, is here to work the games but is also enjoying the tournament as a general basketball enthusiast and, more significantly, a rabid fan of the Syracuse Orange. Roger is breathing easily because Syracuse has defeated the Connecticut Huskies in the first round. Only fifteen minutes ago Syracuse players described the game as a team win, and how everyone played to their potential, and that they were satisfied with the result. Roger, however, describes the contest to me in far more detail as only an informed zealot can. His recall of Syracuse statistics and minutiae is remarkable. When he completes the postgame analysis, I tell him that I am impressed.

"I'm a true fan."

"You are."

"Got a funny story for you."

"You do?"

"This is a funny story. Be good for your book. My wife will never let me forget this. True story."

"All right."

"True story. This will give you an idea of how far gone I am about Syracuse." He pauses and smiles again at a recollection. "You want to hear this story?"

"Yes. Sure. I want to hear the story."

"Okay. The year they won the tournament, two thousand two–three, I got into this thing. Superstitious habit."

"You're superstitious?"

"When it comes to the Orange I will do pretty much anything. This story will illustrate what I am talking about here." He takes a sip of a soft drink before continuing. "Okay. Before the first game of the tournament, I was hungry so I ate two hot dogs just before tip-off. We win the game. So, I remember this before the second game, which is, you know, only two days later.

I figure since we won the first game after I ate the hot dogs—just to be safe—I should eat two hot dogs before this second game also. So, I eat two hot dogs before the game. We win again. Now we have won two games after I have eaten two hot dogs. When the next round starts, I am afraid not to eat the two hot dogs. You know where I am going on this?"

"I think so. I think you're going to be eating hot dogs all through the tournament."

"Well, yeah. But there's more. Okay, so I have been eating these hot dogs, right, but now it is not good enough to only eat the two hot dogs, I have to remember if I put mustard and relish on them, and which I put on first, the mustard or the relish, so that I don't jinx the team by putting on the relish before the mustard, if the last time I put on the mustard before the relish."

"Sure, wouldn't want to jinx the team."

"Yeah, right, make fun. So, I'm fixing these two hot dogs and eating them before the games and we keep winning. Okay, it's the Kansas game. The final, Monday night. I don't know if it is nerves or what. But I develop this horrible stomach ache. Feels like a stomach virus. You know. You ever have one of those? Can't hold anything down. Don't want to eat anything. Can't think of eating anything. Can't even smell food without fearing that you will have to run to the toilet. You must have had this."

"Sure. They're awful."

"Right. Awful. Feel like you're always going to heave."

"Horrible."

"Right. Okay. I have this stomach virus type of thing before the Kansas game. Now I have a problem. You know I am far gone because I think I have this problem."

"What's the problem?"

"The problem is, should I or shouldn't I eat the two hot dogs?"

"You're kidding."

"Not kidding."

"You own your own company?"

He laughs. "Yes, I own my own company."

"Tell me you ate two smelly hot dogs with mustard and relish when you had a stomach virus."

"I ate the hot dogs."

"Took one for the team."

"Took one for the team. Could not let the Orange down."

"You get sick?"

"Got sick."

"Threw up the hot dogs?"

"Threw up the hot dogs. But we won the tournament."

"Must have been the hot dogs."

"Who knows?" says Roger with a smile.

I shake my head incredulously, but I should not have been so astonished. I have known Rogers before.

The next day, I meet a fellow in Mickey Mantle's sports bar on Central Park South. He is dressed in an expensive suit. He tells me that he roots for the Pittsburgh Steelers. Without much in the way of encouragement he tells me that he always bets against the Steelers. I ask him why he always bets against the Steelers if he loves the Steelers.

"When I bet them to win they lose. When I bet them to lose they win. I don't want them to lose, so I bet them to lose, because this way, either way, I win. I win if they win because I've bet them to lose. I win at least money if they lose, because I've bet them to lose. Either way, if I bet them to lose, I win."

No smile accompanies this tortuous explanation, and no vocalizations acknowledge that what he is saying could be convoluted. He relays the rationale as if it is completely rational.

A few days earlier I had been at press row for the finals of the Colonial Athletic Association tournament, watching the

Virginia Commonwealth University Rams play George Mason University. Behind me, in the first row of the arena, was a fanatic who was wearing a hat shaped like a ram's head. He had become a ram for the games. He carried with him a blackboard and scrawled messages for the rest of the crazies in the stadium during time-outs. Near him was a young couple attired head to toe in Virginia Commonwealth University gear. Each partner held a twin baby. The babies were wearing VCU Ram outfits. When Virginia Commonwealth won the thrilling championship game I had good reason to be concerned that I might be trampled to death by the mob of Rams behind me ready to rush the court. If the police had not redirected traffic, many of us on the press level would have been seriously injured by the rush.

The cab driver who took me from my hotel in Richmond to the airport after the tournament was an encyclopedia of information about the University of North Carolina. "What do you want to know?" he asked me. "Ask me anything about the Tarheels. Anything."

I asked him what I thought was a fair question and he responded as if such a test was way too easy for a man who knew what he knew about the Tarheels.

"Don't insult my intelligence. We beat Georgetown in '82 . . . You know my son roots for Duke. Where did I go wrong?" He laughed when he said this, but it seemed to me that he really considered his son's act a betrayal.

During the course of the 2006–2007 season I attended many college basketball games and met zealots at each and every stop. At a Harvard game I sat beside the play-by-play announcer for Boston College basketball games, who was at press row that night not to work but to relax. On my other side was the managing editor of Hoopville.com, a Web site for voracious subscribers who cannot get enough about college basketball. At a Northeastern game I met the color commentator for the Northeastern Huskies, who also does the play-by-play for Harvard games. I was startled at the statistics he could effortlessly recall about the various leagues and players.

In November 2006 I attended the National Communication Association's annual meetings in San Antonio and heard several fascinating papers about the nature of fandom, communication, and the enthusiasm of sports zealots. The most engaging of the papers was delivered by Dr. Rebecca Watts. Her presentation discussed the wild following of the University of Florida football team and how Internet message boards were increasing the fanatical nature of the fans. One supporter of Gator football, she reported, had secured the Web site FireRonZook.com before Ron Zook actually became the coach. This Web site carried communications from concerned supporters who apparently had a crystal ball and knew before the first game that this hire was not good for the Gators. A number of years later Ron Zook was, indeed, fired, and he would eventually be replaced by Urban Meyer. To preclude the discourse of maniacal fans who might not give Urban Meyer a chance, someone secured the site FireUrbanMeyer.com before another crazy could launch a robust virtual conversation intended to oust Meyer before he ever got a chance to succeed.

Eating two hot dogs that will make you sick, wondering about a child's allegiance and parental failure because of a son's affinity for a rival team, betting against your team to secure a win, having uncanny memory for obscure basketball statistics, securing the FireRonZook Web site . . . some people out there are loony about sports.

And I know where a percentage of them congregate each March. They are here at the Imperial Palace, and Bally's and the Venetian, throwing pencils at television sets, screaming obscenities at referees in faraway cities, attempting to use the wisdom they have accrued by virtue of their devotion to predict the unpredictable. And regardless of their degrees of success at this wagering enterprise, most are more than just enjoying the ride.

Disguised as a Responsible Adult

After I watch Mikey explode like the Challenger, I move from the small lounge in the Imperial Palace into the Palace's steep amphitheatre. I find a spot two seats away from a man who is betting the horses as well as the basketball games. My neighbor is tall—at least six-two—and bulky, with broad shoulders and a weightlifter's chest. He has a graying mustache and graying sideburns that extend far lower than what is stylish these days. He wears jeans, a purple T-shirt, and, like so many others in the book, a baseball cap that has been turned backward. Unlike so many others with similarly worn caps, he looks less like a twenty-five-year-old than like the father of a child who may now be twenty-five.

Every five minutes or so, my neighbor lumbers down one side of the steep ramp and returns moments later up another aisle. He has betrayed no hint of a smile in half an hour. Each time he plods up the aisle he is more dour than on the previous lap. I wonder if this man is losing a bundle. After about five of these round-trips I see that his backward cap reads "Albany" above the brim.

We discover that we are not only alums but that we played basketball on freshman Albany teams ten years apart. We discuss university history and our mutual familiarity with school folks and lore. John—"call me Jackie"—is all smiles and no longer somber after only a few minutes of conversation. I suspect his solemn appearance had less to do with his winnings or losings than with the way he sets his jaw when sitting alone.

"Gee," I said, "I thought you were losing more and more of the mortgage money each time you looped back up here. I've seen happier faces in my dentist's waiting room."

He waves me off. "You didn't look like Mr. Happy yourself. 'Who's this guy staring at me,' I'm saying. 'The CIA in town or something?'"

I laugh at myself and wonder how I would be described by someone else writing this type of book.

"You bet on Albany?" I ask.

"Yeah. I bet us on the money line," he said. "I figure we had no chance to get close to Virginia. But if I am wrong I think I could be way wrong, so I bet on the money line thinking maybe we get close and I can make a killing."

"Not to be," I say.

"Not to be is right. What a shellacking." Jackie shakes his head.

"You like the horses?"

"Not really. I mean, I bet the ponies every once in a while, but I don't know what I'm doing. Not that I know what I'm doing with basketball either. I'm down a bundle, but hey," he says, waving his arms around, "this is great. What a collection of junkies."

We both snort in amusement not primarily because we are looking at an assembled collection of junkies, but more because we know that we are among the addicted.

"Some great T-shirts," Jackie says.

We talk about the array of clever T-shirts that are worn by so many. I ask if he has seen the one that reads "Good Coaches Win, Great Coaches Cover."

He nods. "Yeah. Saw that. But that's not my favorite."

"What's your favorite?

"One I saw yesterday is my favorite. You had to see this."

"Good huh?"

"It was great. Guy yesterday. No kid. Guy had to be pushing sixty. Gray hair, much more gray than me. Receding hairline. The gray hair slicked back with some sort of old-time goo. Brylcreem or Sleek or something like that. He's also got this little pony tail going, the kind where there's barely any tail. He has a rubber band around the little stub of hair sticking out. You know what I am saying? You know the look?"

"Sure. Classic look."

"Right. Gray hair slicked back, has this T-shirt. Okay."

"Uh-huh."

"It's this black shirt. White letters. Shirt says this."

Jackie sticks his hand straight out and moves it left to right as if he is pretending to read a headline.

"Disguised as a Responsible Adult."

We both laugh. "I've seen that before. Not yesterday, though."

Jackie is practically in tears. He says it again. "Disguised as a Responsible Adult. Everybody in this joint should be wearing that shirt."

• • •

Jackie's reference reminds me of two years ago, when I was up in the nosebleed section of the Imperial Palace with a buddy and dozens of other tournament bettors. The good news was that we were seated where we had our own TV set. The bad news was that hot air rises, and, that year, it was unbearably hot in the Palace. They have since redone the air conditioning, but then it was a furnace up near the peak of the amphitheater. Nevertheless we had beers in our hands and were focused. We'd hit the buffet earlier, scoured the sheets while consuming the fare, and were ready. We had bet a three-game parlay and were all set to be winners as long as Oakland University, a team from Rochester, Michigan, could get within 28 points of North Carolina. That year Oakland entered the tournament with a losing record, so they figured to be whipped by a power like Carolina, but 28 points is a lot of lumber.

Nevertheless, North Carolina was pummeling Oakland and was up by more than 30 points early in the second half. Oakland was fighting courageously but was clearly overmatched. Those of us who took the dog figured we still had a chance. We assumed that North Carolina up by 30 would put in its substitutes for the last few minutes while Oakland would keep playing its best players in order to look respectable and not be embarrassed by the final score.

However, for reasons that were concurrently puzzling and exasperating, North Carolina was staying with the starters. Periodically, the TV cameras panned the North Carolina bench. The scrubs seated at the end looked as if they all had the same thought: "If we don't get into a game like this, we'll never get in a game." The bettors were as eager as the players for a substitution, but it did not seem as if it would happen. With less than a minute to go in the contest, a fellow two rows in front of us stood up and wailed—practically begging: "PUT THE WHITE GUYS IN!"

It was around then when I saw the shirt "Good Coaches Win, Great Coaches Cover" for the first time. And I began to wonder if there was pressure on coaches to cover from alums or anybody else.

Later that night we went to the very elegant Bellagio Hotel. The sports book was too crowded so we found our way to a bar adjacent to the book where all the games were being displayed. My buddy found a seat at the bar and I was standing behind him. A fellow from Atlanta who had a thick drawl stood next to us. In front of him was a compatriot wearing an Old Dominion baseball cap and a T-shirt that read, "Disguised as a Responsible Adult."

Soon we discovered that the fellow with the Old Dominion cap and the man who hailed from Atlanta had just recently met. They shared perspectives on basketball wagering, loved betting the dogs, and had become instant buddies as they discussed their common interests.

On that night in 2005 Old Dominion was playing Michigan State and getting 9 points. The fellow with the Old Dominion cap who advertised himself as a responsible adult figured wagering on ODU was a sure thing. Atlanta and Old Dominion were spewing advice to anyone in the vicinity, and we were, for better or worse, in the vicinity. Old Dominion had a set of pipes and was broadcasting the fact that all four of the 1 seeds did not cover.

"The dogs, the dogs, the dogs, the dogs," he said with a smile. "Not a single 1 seed," he bellowed—maybe to promulgate his wisdom, but as likely as not because he had been drinking beer while perched at the bar for nine hours—"not a single 1 seed has beaten the spread."

I told him that a 1 seed had in fact beaten the spread. It was North Carolina who, regrettably, waited too long to put in the white guys and therefore defeated Oakland by more than 28 points.

"No they did not," the responsible adult informed me, smiling in a manner that suggested that he believed he was dealing with a simpleton. "No they did not."

Old Dominion proceeded to explain that he also took Oakland but received more than 28 points. His pal from Atlanta piped in and asked when we had placed our bets. We told him that we did so earlier that morning. Again we see a supercilious look. It all but oozed "God made many fools."

"Fellows," Old Dominion said condescendingly "you have got

to place your bets before the stupid money comes to town. The stupid money can fuck with you. It affects the betting line. If more people bet on Oakland that drives the spread down." Old Dominion spreads his arms wide and places his hands palms up. He continues the lecture in a staccato cadence. "You have to bet ahead of the stupid money."

This part of the lesson complete, Atlanta explained another theory he had that involved betting the halftime scores. He liked betting halftime because then he said there would be no slowing down, both teams would still be playing all out, and a bettor would not have to account for the game's "vicissitudes" or a "coach's acumen in the last minutes" affecting the spread. Vicissitudes and acumen in a sports book. Thick-drawl Atlanta spoke confidently but softly. Not his buddy Old Dominion. He was a crass barker in a carnival.

On the television screen, Bucknell, an underdog, was beating Kansas. This simply tickled Old Dominion, as it confirmed once again his "bet the dogs" wisdom. Periodically, he boomed "Buck fucking Nell! "Buck fucking Nell!" Someone in the back of the bar shouted, "Where the fuck is Bucknell?" The response from Old Dominion was blunt, "I don't give a fuck where it is, as long as they cover."

Old Dominion and Atlanta high-fived themselves to exhaustion as Bucknell not only covered but upset Kansas. With Bucknell leading by a single point and only seconds left, Kansas fouled a Bucknell substitute, hoping that the youngster would miss and they would have one more shot at winning. The Bucknell sub walked to the foul line looking as if he was walking to the gas chamber.

"Check out his shorts," boomed the Disguised Responsible Adult with an Old Dominion cap. "Check out his shorts. Gotta be some stains on those shorts."

The obviously nervous sub bricked the free throws, but Kansas could not score in the final seconds, setting off the explosion of high-fives. When Michigan State beat Old Dominion 89–81, failing to cover the 9-point spread by one, Old Dominion was nearly teary-eyed with glee.

It became apparent that, despite his "dog" philosophy, Old Dominion lost big betting on a heavily favored Syracuse team that, inexplicably, not only failed to cover but had lost to Vermont earlier in the evening. This was a minor setback given his other successes, but he felt compelled to deliver a self-deprecating lecture. He stood on the barstool support, turned to the standing patrons, and posed a rhetorical question to nobody in particular.

"How is it possible that a team like Syracuse can win the Big East and then come out and lay an egg like they did against Vermont?"

He shook his head and exhaled a reminder intended for himself: "The dogs, the dogs, the dogs, the dogs."

Old Dominion could not let the Syracuse defeat go. After he finished shaking his head he suddenly wailed in a voice that could have been heard by blackjack players forty yards away.

"It was fucking Vermont," he boomed. "It was fucking Vermont."

This outburst prompted a response on the other side of the bar from someone who sounded as if he too had pitched a tent by the beer taps at 9 a.m.

"Yeah, but it was fucking Syracuse."

After the Bucknell game, my buddy and I walked back across the Strip into Bally's. It was almost nine o'clock, and all the games for the day were nearly over. The scene at Bally's was a janitor's nightmare. The area was littered with empty pizza boxes, half-eaten pizza slices, wax paper with mustard stains, takeout Styrofoam containers with gnawed sparerib bones, empty beer bottles, paper cups, cigar butts, betting line sheets, crumpled parlay cards, and hundreds of losing betting tickets. Several drunken bettors sulked around as well. The drinkers that night had crossed the line from giddy to rude and, particularly if they'd been losing, had become sour and angry.

Among the refuse at Bally's I found a $300 betting ticket for the over at the Bucknell game. The over-under was 127½. The final score was Bucknell 64–Kansas 63, 127 points. The fellow who owned this ticket lost $300 by a half a point. I recalled the nervous Bucknell substitute who had missed the foul shots at the end of the game and wondered if the poor shnook who had this ticket placed his wager after the stupid money came to town.

Where'd You Find the Crab Legs?

Jackie—my fellow Albany alum—and I decide to view the last set of games together in Caesars Palace. Caesars is located directly across the street from the Imperial Palace on the other side of the Strip. However, we are hungry. Neither one of us has consumed much more than beer and pretzels since 9 a.m. So, we decide to "do" a buffet before we watch more of the games.

We have eaten at Las Vegas buffets in past years and spend a few moments debating the merits of this one or that. We factor in location. Jackie says he has eaten at the Garden Buffet before and it filled him right up. Jackie is bigger than I am by at least seventy, and maybe as many as a hundred, pounds. I wonder how overwhelming the Garden Buffet must be to fill him right up. I have some concerns that it might well overwhelm me. Nevertheless, we decide to do the Garden Buffet at the Flamingo, which is just a short walk away.

The buffet at the Flamingo, in fact, does us. When I leave the restaurant I ache. At one point I discover that it is difficult for me to turn one way or another without first making a complete stop. I feel as if I am lugging a Chrysler in my stomach as I slog up and over the pedestrian overpass that leads to Caesars.

●●●

It is hard to describe Las Vegas buffets to the uninitiated. Everyone has been to all-you-can-eat restaurants and has seen and eaten too much. However, thinking beyond reality and indulging in fantasy is foundational to the culture of Las Vegas. And the buffets exemplify this. The sheer quantity and diversity of food at the Garden Buffet was something out of a hungry child's dream. Like so much in Las Vegas, the experience was over the top of even that which we consider to be over the top. At the Garden Buffet, I felt as if I was wandering through a caricaturist's representation replete with exaggerated and distorted depictions of chefs, foodstuffs, and other diners.

The experience began conventionally. Jackie and I were welcomed by a hostess who seated us. Almost immediately a waiter approached our table and took a beverage order. We were then invited to the buffet tables to begin our dinner. After that the experience became unconventional.

The sheer size of the spread was unlike even the most extensive buffet with which I had been familiar. Each section of the tables represented diverse and distinctive cuisines. I visited Little Italy, Chinatown, a Mexican bistro, a steak and rib joint, and a seafood restaurant. I moved to another section and met a chef slicing ham, turkey, and roast beef, banquet style. I continued past him and found pans filled with jambalaya, mashed potatoes, sliced potatoes, sausage and onions, and vegetables of all varieties, many of which I could not identify and suspect I had never seen previously. Another area had bread choices that were beyond plentiful: bagels, rolls, French bread, croissants, rye, wheat, pumpernickel. The spreads and cheeses were similarly diverse. An entire area was dedicated to salads: seafood, tuna, egg, potato, macaroni, tomato, cucumber, potpourri, antipasto. The bowl of tossed greens looked like it was out of place adjacent to the more enticing combinations. Even the Caesar salad seemed like it was too pedestrian to consider, what with the more alluring choices. Continuing past the salads, I discovered a fried food section where I could damage my arteries by consuming fried chicken, fish, steak, potatoes, and hush puppies. Then cold seafood, with clams, mussels, smoked salmon, sushi, herring, crab legs, and a bountiful mound of shrimp resting on ice. If I wanted some soup I could indulge my desires fully with bowls of clam chowder, French onion, cream of mushroom, tomato bisque, and assorted other creations. If I wanted noodles, I could have them with multiple meat, fish, and sauce permutations. Thai food? Indian? I could indulge limitlessly and feel as if my innards would forever be on fire. If I still needed sustenance I could visit a pizza parlor, a hot dog stand, or a faux McDonald's. There was a sub shop where I could obtain any type of hero I requested.

At the end of this disorientating and surreal array was a bakery that offered every sort of pie and cake and cookie and doughnut and strudel and bobka and cream-filled this and that, and even puddings and ice cream sundaes. Those determined to self-deceive could peruse a final section of dietetic pastries.

It was, literally, too much. The buffet table was half a football field of food.

In addition to the enormity of the offerings, I could not help but notice the enormity of some of the patrons. People larger than the largest people I know seemed to travel in herds in the Garden Buffet. Again, I had the feeling that this was not a real experience but rather I had somehow been assigned to observe characters and scenes from a comic book. After Jackie and I had filled our plates and were ready to begin eating, a hostess approached our booth trailed by a family of four that, apparently, was to be seated at the booth directly behind us. There were two teenage children and the parents. The children and the father were enormous, like huge caricatures. The overweight mother looked like a marathon runner compared to the rest of them. They were so heavy that when they sat down in the cushioned booth behind Jackie, I had the strange sensation that I was on a teeter totter and that Jackie and I would be rocketed up to the chandeliered ceiling. As big as they were, their bulk did not preclude several ups and downs to the food counters, and it was easy to see how they maintained their girth. Like everything in Las Vegas they seemed somehow out of proportion. I wondered whether there should be some restrictions on this. Was allowing these people into the buffet akin in some way to serving a double shot of scotch to a regular bar patron who was known to be a wife-beating drunk? Was it similar to conveniently ignoring the truth when a notorious gambling addict placed the rent on Boston College to cover the spread? This family was a heart attack waiting to happen. Did someone have a responsibility to stop them? Or are we obliged to allow anyone the freedom to do what they would like as long as the self-destructive behavior does not directly and immediately affect identifiable others?

Nonbettors during this March Madness season might find another aspect of the dining experience to be peculiar. As I scanned the buffet I counted seven tables populated with bettors who had spreadsheets and notebooks scattered on the tables. Men, often with their mouths full or jaws working industriously, gazed at the printouts, occasionally dropping their forks to scribble greasy notes. At least another half dozen tables were filled with young men who looked the part even if I did not see their betting sheets or notebooks.

One such fellow on his way back from the spread carried a platter stacked with pulled pork, coleslaw, a slab of ribs, a huge cube of baked lasagna, and who knows what on the periphery and underneath. He was very large and wore an oversized football jersey that came down to a point between his waist and knees. He could have been a cousin to the teenagers sitting in the adjacent booth.

He saw Jackie and me reviewing our betting sheets, so he leaned over and said something. Apparently he had not been able to wait until he was seated back at his table before starting to gnaw on a sparerib. The bone moving around in his mouth made him difficult to understand.

I thought he said, "You like Ohio State tomorrow?"

"Say what?" asked Jackie.

I lived in some semblance of a fraternity house while in college and am familiar with unattractive dining habits, but this guy with the sparerib in his mouth was creating a uniquely unappetizing picture as he drooled around his bone, hoping to get an opinion on the Ohio State game. To make himself heard more clearly he did not remove the sparerib. He squatted down like a baseball catcher still holding his stacked plate while treating the sparerib like it was an oversized toothpick.

"You like Ohio State?" he asked again as he moved the bone from one side of his mouth to the other with his tongue.

"We haven't picked tomorrow's games yet," I answered.

He nodded and stood up.

"Ohio State will cover." He offered this prediction as if I had asked him for one. "There's no answer for Oden. Lay the lumber." He paused. "You like Holy Cross tonight?"

Jackie said we had not decided.

"Go with the Cross," he said. He made a face and nodded repeatedly as if to emphasize that betting on "the Cross" was the smart move.

We were grateful that he was apparently ready to return to his table. He turned to go, took a step away from us, and then glanced at my plate. I saw him raise his head and stare sideways at my food. He took the sparerib out of his mouth with his free hand and used the bone to point to my plate. "Hey, where'd you find the crab legs?"

I told him where the crab legs were. He looked at his overburdened plate, thinking.

"Ah, I'll come back for them." he said. But he had not convinced himself and did not move. He continued to mull over the issue. "I'll come back for them," he said again, as if this was important news for me. He replaced the sparerib in his mouth and mumbled again. "I'll come back for it." As he wobbled back to his table he wished us good luck.

• • •

I may have been shocked by the size of the people sitting adjacent to us, but Jackie and I had our share to eat as well.

"You got enough?" I asked Jackie as I pointed to his overflowing plate.

"I won't starve."

"You sure?"

"It'll do for now. You look like you're not getting cheated."

And, indeed, I had not been cheated.

We are in agony as we walk across the Strip to Caesars. Jackie repeatedly wheezes a painful regret: "I did not need that dessert. Did not need the cheesecake."

I feel too full to comment. I need to concentrate on walking.

Blockhead

Caesars Palace is an elegant hotel. Bally's is hardly a dive and the Imperial Palace is similarly fine, but Caesars exudes sophistication. The furnishings are more regal, the guests more aristocratic, and even the staff seems to feel privileged and acts accordingly. As a practical matter, however, this means only that the people losing money in this casino are spending more for the privilege. The hotel room rates are double and triple here what they are in the Imperial Palace, and the minimum bets at the gaming tables are higher than they are directly across the Strip. Nevertheless, very few empty seats are to be found at Caesars' $50 minimum blackjack tables. Other blackjack tables have a minimum bet of $100 a hand, and some have a minimum of $500. At one table the minimum bet is $1,000 a hand. On this Friday night, no blackjack dealers are idle.

The sports book at Caesars is not in an auditorium or amphitheater but, like the book at the Venetian, is situated on the casino floor in an area that has been dedicated entirely to sports and horse race betting. From one side to another the sports book is the length of a football field, much larger than at the Venetian. Twenty rows of comfortable easy chairs have been permanently installed around small round tables in the area closest to the front of the book. Each table has its own television screen so that lounging spectators can switch channels to watch the game of their choice. For this weekend, approximately twenty additional rows of temporary seats have been set up beyond the easy chairs.

A metal railing separates the sports book from a concourse that leads to various other parts of the casino. Tonight, bettors clustered three or four deep behind the rail gaze at six enormous television screens embedded in the walls. These are the largest screens I have ever seen. Each screen measures twelve by fifteen feet and can be easily viewed from behind the distant railing. On both sides of the televisions is an electronic scoreboard that is five times as large as the screens, larger even than the one at Bally's. Below the screens and scoreboards, the more than dozen betting windows look much like cages for tellers at a bank. The queue of bettors clings to the wall and extends, during periods when it is at its longest, well beyond the sports book.

It is really happening tonight in Caesars Palace. Jackie and I survey the scene from behind the masses packed at the railing. We wonder if it was wise to try to view the games here. This enormous space is jammed with bettors, and there seems to be no chance for us to find a place to even stand comfortably, let alone sit. And we do need to sit—we're still wheezing from the buffet at the Flamingo. We decide to try to find two vacant seats. If we can't, we'll haul ourselves back across the Strip because the Imperial Palace ballroom always has some space.

We are far luckier locating open seats at Caesars than either of us has been identifying winning basketball bets. We find two seats together in the very first row of the sports book. These spots are directly in front of the trafficked walkway that separates the betting queue from the first line of prime seats. We are only fifteen feet from the betting counter and so close to the front that we must look directly up to see the viewing screens. Unlike front-row seats in a movie theater, the view of the games from this vantage point is excellent. The only distractions are the pedestrians who continuously pace by. Yet even they do not block our view so much as create peripheral visual turbulence which, after a spell, is only mildly annoying.

Securing these seats would typically require a 4 a.m. wake-up. We discover from the two others around our small table that the seats we now have had in fact been occupied from early in the morning until just moments before our arrival. The previous occupants either ran out of money or just had it.

After we are settled Jackie turns around and stares out behind him.

"Whoa," he says. "Al. You have to check this out."

The site is pure Las Vegas, surreal and fantastic. It seems like thousands of roaring movie extras are sitting and standing behind me, an immense, well-oiled, nearly crazed crowd extending almost as far as the eye can see. Some are cheering, others hoping to cheer. Nearly all hold a betting sheet or notebook. Periodically, booming expletives, assessments, and exhortations can be heard through the din.

"MONEY!"

"Will someone hit a goddamn shot?"

"You have to be kidding with that call!"

"Stuff 'em! Stuff 'em!"

"Jesus!"

"Walking! You sonofabitch. That was a walk."

"Steps? Oh, fuck you!"

"Attaboy. Attababy. Attaboy."

"This is something," Jackie says as he shakes his head.

Something it is. The scene is literally dreamlike, like what I would recall if I were to wake from a dream about Las Vegas. In my dream I would have met wild and distorted characters. I would have heard vulgarities in public places where one typically would not hear such language. I would have seen people incongruously placed in inappropriate venues.

One event in 2006 exemplified such incongruity. I had found a cheap seat in Caesars Palace close to the perimeter railing and had been viewing games on the giant screens. Suddenly something caught my attention in the front of the room: Pete Rose and former UNLV basketball coach Jerry Tarkanian. I had to see them close up to verify that it was really them, so I walked to the front of the room not far from where I am seated now with Jackie. "Charlie Hustle" and "Tark the Shark" were sitting at a table reserved for customer VIPs. These two had spent a good portion of the previous years trying to shed the image that they associated with gambling and gamblers. They chatted amiably, looking every bit like everyone else in the sports book. It wasn't an illusion or a dream. They were there. Just like the wild and wired young men screaming their crass analyses all around Jackie and me.

•••

Over dinner Jackie and I decided to seriously review tonight's games. We would not bet on every game. Our goal was to study the information we had and identify three wagers that we felt were truly locks. We were both graduates of a major university, had advanced graduate degrees, and had played basketball and knew something about the game. We wanted to see if dispassionate analysis could result in three bets that were as close to a sure thing as you could find in a gambling establishment.

Before he left for Las Vegas, Jackie had printed out some information about the teams in the tournament that he had found on the Internet. We studied this information, determined not to be influenced by the tips of the behemoth who had interrupted our meal or the flippant opinion of anyone else we had met. These bets would be strictly our choices based on knowledge and industrious evaluation. Eventually we identified three very solid bets.

The first two were from the same game: Florida–Jackson State. Florida is the reigning NCAA champion, having won last year's tournament. They are a 1 seed in this year's tournament. Jackson State, on the other hand, is not only a 16 seed but according to our analysis, a very weak 16 seed. During the 2006–2007 season

Jackson State did not rank among the top one hundred basketball teams in the country in a single offensive category. Our thinking is that Florida will pummel them, establishing their superiority within minutes and easily covering the halftime spread of 15½ points. Against a team that is so weak offensively the juggernaut that is Florida might be up by as many as 15 points in the first 10 minutes.

However, we know that if Florida wins as expected, they will have to play again on Sunday in the second round of the tournament. Therefore we believe that in the second half Florida will relax and substitute weaker players to rest the better ones for Saturday's game. Given this, we determine that while Florida will cover the halftime spread they will not cover the very large full-game spread of 29 points. There would be no reason for Florida to go all out after having all but secured the victory in the first half. I did remind Jackie of the "put the white guys in" game, when substitutes were not employed until the very end. We went back and forth on this issue, but both of us concluded that Florida would be unlikely to continue pressuring Jackson State in order to sustain a 30-point advantage.

We went through the scenarios over and over and felt we would win these two wagers easily.

Our third bet was another that we liked more and more as we continued to review it. We considered this one to be as close to a guarantee as any wager could be. Holy Cross would be playing the Southern Illinois University Salukis. The over-under was only 109 points. We decide to bet the over. We thought that if either Holy Cross or SIU scored in the 60s, the opponent would have to score less than 50 for us to lose the wager. The winner of a high percentage of college games scores in the 60s. Very few teams score in the 40s, even in defeat. Consequently, it would be difficult for the teams to score collectively fewer than 109 points. If the winner scores 60 and the loser scores 50 we have 110 and win the bet.

In the final pregame analysis we feel very good about our wisdom. It seems to us that if you can discipline yourself not to bet on all games and do not bet capriciously, intelligence and industry can be applied to whittle down the variables so that some games become predictable.

•••

The two others seated around our small table look drugged, as if they have been in their seats consuming alcohol for seventeen hours. This, we discover, is because that they have in fact been sitting in these seats consuming alcohol for seventeen hours. Nevertheless, before we get on the queue to place our very sure bets we ask our anesthetized neighbors for their opinion.

Neither of these fellows is particularly friendly or supportive. One of them answers with a shrug that seems to say "I'm too tired to care" or "Who the hell knows." The other offers a four word assessment.

"You two are fucked," he says.

We cannot decide if this grump is commenting on the two of us in general or if this is a prediction of our chances for success. Regardless, the analysis is not encouraging. We reconsider our logic but decide to stick with the plan. Jackie reviews the bets.

"Florida and Jackson State should not be on the same court. Florida goes out fast and then will not run it up."

I nod in agreement. Jackie continues.

"We are in good shape with the hundred and nine over. Two high school teams could combine for a hundred and nine points in thirty-two minutes. Two college teams will never score less than a hundred and nine in forty minutes."

We smack hands with each other on these can't miss bets.

"We'll see who's fucked, pal," says Jackie, who has a master's degree and an educational certificate in guidance and counseling psychology. "We'll see who's fucked."

I get on the betting queue while Jackie saves our seats. After a spell, a fellow behind me on the line pokes me. He wants to know how to bet. As I did earlier with the woman from Ohio State I explain the basics of placing a wager. I tell him that when he gets to the window he should identify the number of the team that he wants to bet on and the amount of the wager.

"So," I continue, "let me give you an example. Who are you betting on?"

"Not sure yet," he says.

We are only three people away from the window when he tells me this.

"But I get it," he continues. "Just say the number and the amount of the bet. Right?"

"Right," I say and turn around.

A moment later the same fellow taps me again.

"How much should you bet?" he asks. "I mean what's normal? What's the minimum?"

I tell him that the minimum in Caesars is $10.

"Ten dollars?" he says incredulously and laughs. "Ten dollars? Who would only bet ten dollars? I'm betting at least a hundred."

"Oh. Okay. Who you betting on?"

"Told you. Not sure yet."

I place our wagers and move to the side to put the change and tickets back into my wallet.

The novice goes to the window I've vacated. With confidence he bets $100 on Florida to cover and $100 for Southern Illinois to cover the 7-point spread against Holy Cross.

I tell Jackie this story when I return to our seats.

"That's two hundred out the window," he says.

I nod my head in agreement. "What a blockhead. Imagine that. Two hundred dollars out the window. The guy did not have a clue. Did not know how to bet. Did not know how much to bet, but he bets two hundred dollars without thinking about it."

I take out our betting slips while still shaking my head. Jackie looks at the tickets. He notices something.

"The Holy Cross–Southern Illinois over went to one-thirteen."

I study the ticket. Jackie is right. Apparently the stupid money has come in and pushed the over up by 4 points.

"I should have checked that," I say. "Sorry."

"Don't worry," says Jackie. "We'll still cover the over. And besides, we can't miss with the Florida bets."

●●●

Somehow we manage to. Instead of coming out like a ball of fire, Florida begins the game flat and Jackson State, despite the inferior pedigree, competes effectively. Florida leads at the half, but only by 6 points, not 15. We have lost our first can't miss lock—the halftime bet.

We consider this initial loss but are not terribly distressed. We figure that the way Jackson State is playing we're a cinch to win the full-game wager. Florida is certainly not going to come out and beat Jackson State by more than 29 points now. At least we will break even.

We are incorrect a second time. Florida must have been upset by its weak play. Jackson State must have figured they had done enough by staying close in the first half. At the start of the second half Florida plays like a defending champion that is furious and Jackson State plays like a team that does not rank in the top one hundred in the nation in any offensive category. In the second half Florida butchers Jackson State, winning not by 29 points but by 43. We have now lost our second can't miss bet.

We are certainly not elated by our failures but we know we still have the Holy Cross–Southern Illinois over. How difficult will it be for these teams to score 113 points put together?

It proves to be close to impossible. Neither Southern Illinois nor Holy Cross can drop a dime in the Grand Canyon. Both teams look like they could not get through a layup drill without losing the ball somewhere. After a particularly ugly set of turnovers, a fellow from way in the back bellows so loudly that even in the front I feel as if I might need to hold my hands to my ears. In the first of several pronouncements this man screams, "HOW CAN YOU COACH A TEAM TO BE SUCH SHIT?"

Jackie and I laugh but feel the same. We start doing mathematical proportions to consider our chances. If the teams have scored X points in 29 minutes, how many points will they score in 40 minutes when the game is over? It is folly to do this, as events in the last 5 minutes of a game alter the scoring pace, but we do it anyway.

The game is a close one, but how close it may be is of no consequence to us as we just need the total points to be greater than 113. We just want someone, anyone, to score. And apparently not a single player on either team is capable of placing the ball inside the basket. When Southern Illinois begins to distance itself from Holy Cross, fans start a Salukis cheer. The cheer and cheering does not help.

The same screamer yells again: "YOU GUYS ARE TERRIBLE!"

Neither team can make a foul shot or a field goal. As a review of the final game statistics would reveal, a player for Holy Cross will make only 3 of 16 field goal attempts. A Southern Illinois player will shoot 2 for 9.

Jackie and I are groaning with every miss. With 1 minute to play the score is 61–47, Southern Illinois. A total of 108 points. We need 113. Holy Cross makes a layup to bring the score to 61–49, 110 points. There is hope. On the subsequent possession, Southern Illinois manages, and not by any stretch for the first time, to lose control of the ball before attempting to take a shot. Holy Cross gains possession and scores a 2-point goal with 27 seconds to play. The score is now 61–51, 112 points. There are still 27 seconds to play. We need 113. All we need is one basket.

It is agony to watch these seconds.

Southern Illinois does not have to shoot and attempts to run out the last 27 seconds. Again the voice from the back: "FOUL, YOU HOLY CROSS BASTARDS!"

To the joy of half the people in the sports book, and the agony of the other half, Holy Cross gives up. Holy Cross figures it cannot overcome a 10-point deficit in 27 seconds. Southern Illinois dribbles the ball without molestation for the remainder of the game.

"YOU HOLY CROSS BASTARDS! YOU DON'T FOUL? THERE'S A HALF MINUTE LEFT. HOLY CROSS? HOLY SHIT, NOT HOLY CROSS!"

We have lost all three of our intelligent, rational, can't miss bets.

"Told you, you were fucked," says our drugged neighbor.

As Jackie and I are gazing at the losing betting slips, the novice goofball I'd met on the line passes by. He is returning from the cashier's window after collecting his winnings. Florida has covered the 29-point spread and Southern Illinois University has similarly covered, defeating Holy Cross by 10 when the spread was only 7. This beginner, who hours ago did not even know how to place a bet, has won $200. He spots me and looks giddy.

"Hey, thanks a lot," he says as he slaps a wad of bills against my shoulder. "Thanks a lot. Thanks for your help. This is great."

He flashes me the peace sign as he bounds away. I mutter "Peace" in response with no small amount of sarcasm. Jackie and I spent an hour analyzing the data, identified three sure bets, and lost all three. This blockhead capriciously makes a selection thirty seconds before he gets to the betting window and wins $200. Who is the blockhead?

•••

A photographer from the *New York Times* is taking photos of the Caesars Palace sports book scene. He tells me that the *Times* will be running a story next week about March Madness.

"Pretty crazy, right?" he asks me.

"Pretty crazy," answers Jackie, but he sounds subdued.

Jackie says good night. He has had it. I stick around in the great seats at Caesars Palace. I decide I need a winner and try to bet the pro games. I take the Lakers, and Kobe Bryant saves my day by scoring 65 points. I need all of them as the Lakers win in overtime and beat the spread.

•••

After Kobe finally makes me something of a winner for the evening, I begin my walk out of Caesars toward the Imperial Palace. As I leave I see something that is again surreal Las Vegas. In the middle of the casino, near the roulette wheel and blackjack tables, two stages have been erected. They are right in the center of armies of pedestrian traffic. Both stages have a caged periphery. Long poles have been secured to the platforms. Within the cages attractive young women are dancing and writhing to music as they place themselves on and around the poles. They are wearing some clothing but not much. Essentially, Caesars is using an upscale, but nonetheless steamy, floor show to lure customers. It is no wonder Mike Fay described Las Vegas this weekend as a huge fraternity party.

• • •

As I approach the entrance to the Imperial Palace I am startled by a man waiting in line for a cab with his sweetheart. Her arm is around his waist and his arm is around her shoulders. They are standing close together near the curb. She does not seem to be a professional. She looks to me to be the man's wife or girlfriend.

The man, in his thirties, is wearing a T-shirt that has an obscene message on it. It is well beyond bad taste. It is revolting. I have seen many items these past two days that are in bad taste, but this is the most vulgar, repulsive, appalling T-shirt I have ever seen. Yet this man is standing with his arm around his mate—who herself is conventionally attractive and attired—waiting calmly for a cab as if he is wearing a sports jacket and tie.

Two questions come to mind: What type of person would wear such a shirt? What type of woman would be seen, let alone cuddle, with a man who would wear this shirt?

I look around at the others waiting on the cab line. Maybe they have already noticed this shirt, but no one on the line or among the legion walking in and out of the Imperial Palace seems to be startled by what this man is wearing. We are in Las Vegas, and nothing appears to be outside the sphere of normalcy.

• • •

Up in the sports book at the Imperial Palace, halfway up the steep amphitheater, I find the genius from North Carolina. At this late hour, only a dozen other people are left in the entire auditorium, but the genius is sitting several rows up in his "This seat is taken" spot.

"Hey!" I shout. "How are you doing?"

He waves at me. He apparently does not want to get into it. He is drinking a Heineken and looking at Saturday's sheets.

"Bet the money line on Xavier," he barks without looking up, then returns to silence and his homework.

"They didn't come here to lose," I say.

"Damn right," he snaps, still not raising his head.

I feel like I should go to sleep so I take the escalator down to the main floor and walk toward Bette Midler dealing blackjack. I recently finished reading *Bringing Down the House,* so I stop and stand by a blackjack table where Bette has relieved Little Richard and try to count cards at the table. I do not have much success.

I leave Bette Midler. Tomorrow is another day.

An Amusement Park

It is 7:20 a.m. on a brilliant St. Patrick's Day Saturday in Las Vegas. From the balcony of my room at the Imperial Palace I can see the spectacular mountain backdrop beyond the skyline of the Strip. The Imperial Palace is designed in a U shape, so I can see the balconies of many of the rooms across the way.

On an adjoining wing of the hotel a young man wearing only boxer shorts is leaning over a balcony railing. He is thin and appears to be contemplative. In his left hand he is holding what looks like one of the thousands of sports book betting sheets I have seen in the three days I have been in town. In his right hand he holds a bottle of beer.

I need to take a different path. Coffee seems to be the appropriate drug for me at this hour so I decide to go to a Starbucks in the neighboring Harrah's Hotel. Down in the lobby I am welcomed by the now-familiar sounds of the casino. Sammy Davis Jr. is dealing blackjack. Two sleepy women are parked in front of slot machines, robotically pulling the levers and ignoring the diluted screwdrivers in front of them. Occasionally they reach into a bucket that sits between them to find the change that will allow them to keep their machines moving.

I take the serpentine walkway that leads away from the main entrance of the Imperial Palace and winds through the rear of the hotel. It ends at a doorway that opens onto an outdoor corridor to a seldom-used monorail stop. This outdoor corridor also links the Imperial Palace to Harrah's. I pass the monorail entrance, walk through Harrah's, and locate the Starbucks.

Only two customers are ahead of me, but the pace of the attendant is excruciatingly slow, or at least seems to be with the head I've earned from consuming beer nearly constantly for the past forty-eight hours. The customer at the head of the line wants a coffee concoction that sounds extraordinarily exotic, and the Starbucks employee just doesn't seem to get it. "You want cinnamon on the whipped cream, or in the coffee? I'm not sure I understand, ma'am." The person directly in front of me keeps turning around as if to say, "Can you believe how long this is taking?" I want to scream before it is my turn. Finally, I pay the $2.50 for my small plastic container of coffee.

As I drink my coffee I cannot help but overhear a man on a cell phone.

"Ron, listen. I'd like you to consider some tech stocks or funds . . . No. I don't like the pharmaceuticals. I just don't feel good about them. There's too much of a down side, too much risk . . . Yes, I know that several have done well. Hey, they might continue to do well, but eventually if there is some crisis . . . I don't know. I think there is a risk there you need not take . . . I would stick with the techs. EMC, Cisco, SunMicro. Yes, they have taken hits, but I think they are back. In the long run, I love them. I love Cisco in particular. Everybody needs high tech, Ron. Individuals, companies. That is the way to go, in my opinion."

I have only an elementary knowledge of the stock market and little interest in it, but I am struck by how similar this financial advice is to what I have been hearing all weekend as pundits of a different ilk have been "loving" Florida, Memphis, and North Carolina. How much difference is there between betting on tech stocks and betting on North Carolina?

• • •

The stage for improvisational comedians at Harrah's has apparently been transformed into a sports book for this weekend. This is a relatively small sports book. The small cabaret-style tables can hold no more than two hundred people comfortably. Nevertheless, the conversation and action is robust and the noise level is considerable. On what would be the performer's stage is a long counter behind which sports book employees take customers' wagers on today's contests. Thirty-two teams are left in the big dance. Sixteen will play today, and the remaining teams will be on stage tomorrow. Throughout the sports book this Saturday morning, bettors cluster together, considering the eight games on today's slate.

A young man of about twenty-five is leaning over a counter near where the betting sheets are displayed. He is studying the spreads and occasionally scribbling notes. When I get closer to his sheet I see that he has made a list of the teams that he likes and the dollar amounts he intends to wager on them. I discover that he is an intern—a doctor in training—who comes to Las Vegas annually for this weekend. He is staying at the Bellagio with seven undergraduate buddies, all sleeping in the same room.

"Bellagio?" I say. "Very nice."

"We get a room with two double beds. The rooms are expensive, but if you divide it by seven, it's not so bad. We bring sleeping bags and pillows and each night take turns sleeping on the beds."

"Still, sounds crowded."

"Yeah, well. It's a weekend. Besides who stays in the room? I've been playing poker all night."

He then proceeds to tell me, self-effacingly, about how he has become interested in poker because of the exposure the game has recently had on television.

"I watched it on ESPN. I got hooked."

"If you're hooked," I say, "it's a good thing you are going to be a doctor."

He smiles. "Not what you think. You play smart, and you play long enough, you don't lose a lot of money. Sure, you'll probably lose some, but if you use your head you won't spend the rent, and besides it's fun. If you enjoy playing, well, you pay for the entertainment. You go on a ride in an amusement park, you pay for the ride. Lose some money playing poker, you're sort of paying for the ride. That's what this place is," he says, "an amusement park."

"You played all night?"

"Yeah," he snorts. "Going to take a nap in a few minutes but wanted to get some bets down before I go to the room." He pauses a moment. "You like Louisville?"

We talk for a few minutes about the day's games. He tells me he can guarantee a winner. This I have heard before, several times, so I roll my eyes.

"No, seriously, I am telling you. There is no way UCLA–Indiana covers the over. No way. It's a hundred and twenty-seven points. Both those teams play very good defense. I am telling you, that is a lock. I cannot believe the over is one-twenty-seven. Weber State averages something like seventy points a game, and UCLA held them in the forties on Thursday. Gonzaga scores in the seventies, Indiana holds them to fifty-seven on Thursday. This over-under is like stealing."

If this young man is studying anatomy the way he has studied the teams in this tournament I want him to be my physician. He is also a likable fellow, inserting self-deprecating remarks as he presents his handicapping suggestions. Even though his is one of the fifty-some-odd tips I have heard this weekend—many of which have steered me the wrong way—I decide to trust the doctor and bet on this under.

He says he is going to place his bets and take his nap so he waves goodbye and gets on the betting queue. The UCLA–Indiana game will not be played until 5:15, and before I join the line I have other contests to review. I find a seat in the lounge-turned-betting parlor. Nearby, a table of men puff stinky, but I suspect expensively stinky, cigars. They are either oblivious or uncon-cerned that their seats clearly are marked with the words "No Smoking." The men have basketball and horse betting sheets spread in front of them. They look to be in their mid-forties and are not chatting so much as blurting out words as they review their mission for the day.

"Xavier, yes or no?"

"No."

"Why?"

"Got a feeling."

"He had a feeling yesterday too, Murray."

"Ohio State is too tough."

"Is it still at seven and a half?"

"Still seven and a half."

"Don't know."

"Forget Xavier."

"Ohio State."

"Okay, Ohio State. Now, Butler. Yes or no."

Beyond this group some passionate Ohio State bettors are decked out in Buckeye caps, shirts, and in one case basketball shorts that look very much like long boxer underwear. One middle-aged man has a ridiculous lid that looks like a combination of a beret and a chef's hat, rising over his head and sagging by one ear. He is conversing in earnest with others in the group. I wonder how he expects anyone to take his advice seriously in that hat.

Ohio State plays the first game of the day. They are a 7½-point favorite over a Xavier team that, as I painfully remember, defeated Brigham Young by only 2 points on Thursday night when I needed 2½.

The facts suggest that this game will not be much of a contest. Of the sixteen teams in the South Region, Ohio State is ranked first and Xavier ninth. During the regular season, Xavier competed in the Mid-American Conference, a league that is referred to as a "mid-major," a good league but considered not nearly as strong as a major conference such as the Big Ten. Xavier got into the tournament by virtue of an "at large" bid: they lost their conference championship, but the selection committee felt they warranted inclusion. So, Xavier was perceived as worthy of an invitation but did not even win its mid-major conference. In contrast, Ohio State has a record of 30–3 and was automatically invited into the tournament as the champions of the powerful Big Ten.

Ohio State should pummel Xavier and easily cover the 7½-point spread. At least that seems to be the sentiment in Harrah's, not only from the folks decked out in Buckeye gear but also from the experts smoking strong cigars. I am aware of the prevailing sentiment and the data, but am also aware of how well Jackie and I fared with our cerebral analyses last night. Nevertheless, I decide to go with Ohio State even though it would be intuitive at this point to bet counterintuitively.

The betting queue at 8:30 is too long for me, and while the coffee has perked me up, I don't have the energy or patience to wait on it. I know the lines are unlikely to get smaller, but the game is some time off and I figure that I might be able to place a bet at one of the smaller casinos after a spell. The prospect of not being able to do so does not overwhelm my desire to avoid trudging inch by inch to the front of this long betting queue.

I leave the sports book and stroll out into the casino. The craps game is active, and the roulette wheel has more than a few takers. I pause at the blackjack tables. One can lose a good deal of money in a short period of time playing blackjack. Nevertheless, I am tempted to join a table where the minimum bet is $10. I debate the wisdom of taking a seat. I know that I am likely to be short of cash quickly. I rationalize that I am doing research and ease into a chair.

The blackjack table has room for six players who sit in a semicircle facing the dealer. My seat is near the middle, the fourth seat from the right. The seat to my immediate left and two seats to my immediate right are vacant. To my far left sits a woman who looks like she has been there all night. She has some weight on her and wears a sour expression. Near her betting chips is a Bloody Mary that she stirs nearly continuously with two swizzle sticks. The woman, Abby, tells me she cannot catch a break. This self-analysis, however, does not seem to prevent her from sticking around.

The fellow to the extreme right I recognize immediately as a basketball bettor. I've never seen him before but he wears the right duds and has placed a betting sheet in front of him along with his chips. He hasn't shaved in a while, and my guess is that he hasn't been sleeping much, either. He's halfway through a Corona and is chewing on the lime rind from the bottle when I try to engage him. His name is Pete, and looks like he can't be over twenty-two.

"You like Xavier?" I ask.

"Fuck Xavier."

"Like blackjack?"

"Fuck blackjack. I'm just waiting for the games to start."

Pete is not a schmoozer.

I am out $50 before I know it. Betting $10 a game, it would take me all day to lose $50 on basketball games. Abby is hitting on 16 with the dealer showing a 3, taking the cards that would bust the house. She continues to whine that she cannot catch a break. Her husband, she tells me, is a basketball nut. He is here with his "old fart" college friends somewhere. She cannot understand how he can watch basketball all day long.

I tell her that I am doing the same thing.

"You're all crazy," she tells me as she splits a pair of jacks.

By the time I pull myself away from the blackjack table I am down $70. Like many fine academics I have "conducted research" to prove what I knew before I began the study. I have the data to prove that one can lose money very quickly playing blackjack.

● ● ●

Predictably, the lines at the sports book have gotten longer. Only one game begins at 10 today, Xavier–Ohio State. Others begin at 12:20. I will not make it to the front of the line by 10, but I'm sure I'll have time during the first game to place bets on the next bunch.

I decide to watch Xavier–Ohio State in the Imperial Palace ballroom, where I know I will be able to find a seat near a television. I leave Harrah's figuring that my trip here for a tall coffee has set me back $72.50, a high price for a morning beverage even at Starbucks. However, I did meet Abby, Pete, an aspiring physician, a stockbroker, a fellow with a ridiculous hat, and a table of guys smoking expensive cigars. As the poker-playing intern suggested, in an amusement park, you have to pay for the ride.

Jake

On the escalator at the Imperial Palace are two college-age men who, while not the same Ohio State people I saw in Harrah's, are similarly adorned in Buckeye paraphernalia. It is 9:50, ten minutes before the game. One Buckeye is lugging a thirty-pack of Bud Light while another has his arms filled with bags from McDonalds. In the ballroom they head for their similarly clad friends seated at a table and distribute drink and food. Judging from the way they grab at the McDonald's bags and furiously open the sandwiches, these boys are nothing short of ravenous.

There's an empty chair at the table and I ask if I can join them. One fellow with a mouthful counts the chairs while his jaws keep moving. Out of a tiny vacant space from the side of his mouth he mumbles something to the others that sounds like, "How many we got?"

Now several members of the contingent begin to point and count the chairs around the table.

"Is Bonkers coming?" asks Jake. Jake is the name, I discover, of the one who hauled the beer up the escalator.

Someone waves a no and adds an explanation. "Bonkers is still drunk."

The man with the mouthful is still chewing but nearly ready for his next bite. He points to the chair, shrugs his shoulders, and contorts his face, meaning a mix of "Who knows?" and "Knock yourself out." I sit down with the starving Buckeyes.

● ● ●

Some sports fans occasionally suggest to their friends that they put some money on a game to "make it interesting." My sense always has been that the game itself is interesting, and that betting does not render the viewing more exciting. In fact, I think betting can make the game less exciting, especially if you have affection for a particular team. If you support a team that is a favorite, then a bet requires that you not only win but cover. If your team is an underdog, a bet might make a fan care less about a team's victory and more about the team simply getting close. Betting against a spread creates a different game than the ostensible one, and the real game may become less interesting if betting is important to you.

I wonder, however, if my experience this year at March Madness will change my perspective. I have no bet on the Ohio State game and no allegiance to either team, and I predict I will still enjoy watching the contest. As it turns out my prediction is correct. It is difficult to imagine how any true fan would have required a bet to enjoy this game and many of the others that will be played today. However, I also wonder if I am the norm or an anomaly.

•••

My seat for this game provides great entertainment. I'm sitting with Jake and the starving Ohio State breakfast beer guzzlers, but a couple of steps away from us is a table of bettors who have wagered a bundle on Xavier. This other group is not from Cincinnati (where Xavier is located), nor do they go to school at Xavier. They have simply bet on Xavier and need the Musketeers to get within 7½ of Ohio State. My boys with the beer are recent Ohio State graduates. They not only want their alma mater to win, but they need the Buckeyes to win by 8 to collect on their wagers. The battle between these two groups is terrific theater.

As the game progresses the genius from Raleigh, North Carolina, indeed looks like a sage. Just before I went to bed last night he had suggested that I bet the money line on Xavier. It appears that I would have made a good deal of money if I had. Xavier is playing very well, competing as if they belong with their heavily favored opponents from Columbus and in the second half take a lead.

The dedicated Ohio State fans in the Imperial Palace are imploding. Their 1-seeded Buckeyes seem destined not only to fail to cover the 7½-point spread, they may be eliminated from the tournament altogether. My tablemates—with or without Bonkers—are spewing volcanically. Every once in a while one fellow in particular—an enormous young man with a scarlet Buckeye football jersey that nearly but not completely covers his girth—expresses his discomfort with something just a notch short of violence. This man, whose sobriquet must be "Boom" or "Bam" judging from overheard conversation, regularly slams the table so hard that empty beer cans hop up and topple over.

Another in the group—Jake the beer mule—periodically turns around from the television screen and looks at the others at the table. At these junctures Jake holds his hands out to his side like an evangelical preacher about to implore a congregation to repent. His subsequent words, however, are not from the good book. Hands open, pained expression, Jake moans a rhetorical question: "Are you fucking kidding me?"

Jake says this nine times during the game. He has more in his repertoire than this recurring inquiry. Another regular comment concerned his assessment of the officiating: "They are not calling anything. It's a fucking football game out there."

At the same time the Buckeyes at my table are moaning, the Xavier fellows are popping up and down as if their seat cushions have springs. In a particularly incongruous scene, one of them, a young rooter wearing a turban, leaps up and slaps high fives with his comrades again and again.

Ohio State makes a comeback worthy of a 1 seed, giving hope

to Jake and Boom and the rest at my table. With 20 seconds remaining Ohio State has the ball and is behind by only 2 points, 61–59. The Buckeyes have an opportunity to either win the game with a 3-point shot or tie it with a 2-point shot, which will send the game into overtime.

Someone unfamiliar with the nuances of March Madness wagering would assume that Jake, Boom, and their associates would prefer a successful 3-point shot to a successful 2-point shot. With a 3-pointer, Ohio State would win 62–61, and the now well-oiled tribe of supporters around me would rejoice. However, while there would be some joy if that were to occur, this scenario is not what my wagering tablemates are hoping for. They do not want a successful 3-point goal that will result in a win.

Jake, Boom, and the rest of the Buckeyes want a 2-point shot that will result in a 61–61 tie, sending the game into a 5-minute overtime period. Then Ohio State will have a chance not only to win but, significantly, to cover the 7½-point spread.

The Xavier bettors want Ohio State to go for 3. If Ohio State makes a 3, the score would be 62–61, and Xavier would lose the game but beat the 7½-point spread. If Ohio State misses a 3, the score would remain 61–59, and the Xavier bettors would also win—even on the money line.

To the dismay of Jake and the rest, Ohio State takes a 3-pointer with 20 seconds remaining. They miss the shot. The crowd around me erupts in baleful groaning and ecstatic screeching.

After the missed shot a wild scrum breaks out near the basket as both teams war for the rebound. Xavier gains possession, and the Buckeye fans scream that Xavier has committed a foul during the scramble.

A foul against Xavier would be great for Ohio State bettors: Ohio State would get two foul shots. If they were successful, the game would be tied 61–61 and probably go into overtime. During the scrum, however, no foul is called.

"Are you fucking kidding me?" Jake shouts as he stands up, throws his arms forward, and hurls the invective at one of the large television sets in the room. He whips his head around and says, "These guys aren't calling anything. That's a fucking football team out there." Then he collapses, wheezing his refrain, "Are you fucking kidding me?"

The Xavier rooters have their own complaint. After the Musketeer player secured the rebound, he was absolutely pulverized by the main stud for Ohio State, Greg Oden, who is nineteen but looks more like twenty-nine. Oden made the foul to stop the clock: If Xavier misses their free throws, Ohio State would get the ball again with a chance to win or tie.

Oden's foul is so hard that the turbaned Xavier fan bounds up again and screams something I can't understand.

Boom is not bothered by the violence and simply mutters, "Nice mugging."

Someone on the other side of the ballroom screams, "Oden's a sham!"

A fellow at the Xavier table screams, "Fuckin' A!"

Another Xavier bettor walks over to my table as if to plead his case. "Come on," he says to the Buckeyes, "come on, that was a shit call." He is waved away.

I realize that the turbaned Xavier fan is shouting "Intentional!" An intentional foul awards the fouled team two foul shots and control of the ball after the shots are taken. This would almost undoubtedly make Xavier bettors winners.

Over this cacophony, someone in the middle of the arena gets up and bellows, "The Big Ten sucks!"

"Fuck you!" screams my neighbor Jake.

To the dismay of the Xavier supporters, the referee does not call an intentional foul. Nevertheless it still looks good for Xavier and bleak for Ohio State. Xavier will get two foul shots. If both are made the lead will be 63–59, and the game, for all practical purposes, will be over. If only one is made Ohio State will be losing 62–59 and have to race up the court in 9 seconds and make a miracle 3-pointer to tie the game. Even if neither foul shot is made, Ohio State will still have to make a basket in 9 seconds.

The Xavier player makes the first shot but misses the second. A Buckeye player drives up to the 3-point line. With the aid of an egregious moving pick he finds himself open. He hurls up a desperation shot. As time expires the 3-pointer goes through the net to tie the game at 62.

The Imperial Palace explodes. The fellows at my table rifle up in unison, sending empty beer cans flying all over the place. One of the Xavier fans sits with his hands on top of his head repeating, "I cannot believe it. I cannot believe it." The turbaned man is frozen. One of his more vocal compatriots stands up, spreads his arms, and bellows, "Tell me that wasn't a moving pick! Tell me that wasn't a moving pick!" Then he walks over to talk to me, as if I am some kind of levelheaded arbiter.

"Tell me that wasn't a moving pick."

"Aw, shaddup," says Jake. "They're not going to call that shit. It's a fucking football game out there."

In the overtime Xavier is folding but not quite enough for my table buddies from Columbus. While buoyed by what appears to be imminent victory, they still need 7½ points to make their payday. With only a few seconds left Ohio State leads by 7, 76–69, and is on the foul line for two shots. The Ohio State player makes the first shot, which sends up a roar at my table. He makes the second foul shot, and the Buckeye bettors are delirious, as Ohio State is up by 9. The Buckeye fans stand and rally the defense to prevent a disastrous last-second goal by Xavier. It doesn't work. With 8 seconds left, Xavier makes a meaningless putback layup, reducing the lead to 7. The Ohio State bettors flop to the table like a bunch of ducks that have been shot.

The game ends. Ohio State wins, 78–Xavier 71, but Xavier beats the spread by half a point. The Xavier table erupts in wild cheering. The Ohio State table sags limply in their seats.

"Are you fucking kidding me?" says Jake.

"Well," I say, "at least you won."

The bunch of them stare at me as if they are all thinking, "What planet could this guy be from?"

It is time for me to leave. Over at the Xavier table, the man in the turban is doing the victory mambo.

Where Are the Damn Sheets?

After the Ohio State game I go to the area where the betting sheets are laid out in the sports book amphitheater of the Imperial Palace.

An angry-looking man with a half-empty cigarette pack popping out from the sleeve of his T-shirt is trying to find the basketball betting sheets. He looks like he might be forty, came to Las Vegas from somewhere local to score needed money, and has just lost the rent—an example of how the joy is not always there in betting.

He moves truculently to where the basketball sheets are usually stacked but doesn't find them. He scatters the irrelevant sheets for hockey, professional basketball, baseball spring training, golf, arena football, and NASCAR as so much litter. He needs the college basketball sheets and he needs them now.

He pushes the inconsequential papers aside and barks, "Where are the damn college basketball sheets?" He spots me and, as if his fury justifies demanding information from anyone in the vicinity, asks me, "Where are the damn sheets?"

"I don't know."

"You don't know. You don't fucking know."

He shakes his head and stares at me as if some people get all the breaks and he, somehow, always winds up getting screwed. I begin to wonder if what he truly seeks is not the sheets but a brawl. He is so obnoxious that I have a desire to confront him, but a fight with him will result in the both of us being expelled. I walk away, making a note that March Madness is not always fun for everyone.

This man's behavior can fuel the argument that Las Vegas during March Madness—or at any time—is an iniquitous haunt that breeds undesirable people and irresponsibility. This notion is at odds with my experience and, I believe, represents an illogical if not dangerous extrapolation.

In gambling as in other activities there are extremes. Encounters with angry bettors, encounters with inebriated bettors, and encounters with people apparently betting far too much than they can afford do not mean that these people depict the norm. Most of the people I have met during March Madness weekends were having fun and no more likely to evolve into self-destructive gambling addicts than the fellow who stops at the neighborhood pub for a pint is likely to become the town drunk. Most people would not assume that someone who drinks a beer at night is an alcoholic, or those who occasionally enjoy a piece of cheesecake are problem eaters, or those who enjoy consensual intimacy are sex addicts.

Without the lure of Las Vegas, the furious man I encountered might not be in the dire condition he appears to be in, but irresponsibility is not the inevitable result of gambling, or eating, or drinking—it is the inevitable result of individual behavior, choices, and excesses. The identification of gambling as ineluctably linked to depravity can be dangerous, as it might deflect attention away from other more legitimate sources of societal corrosion, such as communal acceptance of deception and duplicity.

•••

Gambling on games, of course, can fuel illegal activities that can have devastating consequences on sports. Criminals have attempted to engineer the final outcome of games in order to reap a profit by "gambling" on a sure thing. Nothing is more central to the foundation of sports than fans assuming that a game is being played honestly. Remove that premise and fan enthusiasm, media interest, and advertising revenue evaporate.

Gangsters have influenced college (and to a lesser extent professional) basketball players to "fix" games. In the early fifties, sixties, and eighties some of these conspirators were exposed, caught, and punished. In 2007 a professional basketball official was convicted of attempting to affect the scores of games.

College athletes are especially susceptible to approaches by criminals who tell them that their involvement will be minimal, the rewards great, and the offense relatively insignificant. Because so many bets are made against a spread, a gangster could argue that a player would not have to do anything detrimental to his team to realize a substantial reward. All the player would have to do would be to "shave" some points—that is, deliberately reduce the differential between the winning and losing team in order to cover the spread. For example, if the spread is 12 points and a player's team is winning by 11, what is the harm in missing two meaningless foul shots at the end of the contest, or throwing away a pass, or allowing an opponent easy access to the basket? The player's team would still win, and the conspirator could come away with a good deal of money. No one would get hurt. Everybody wins.

These arguments are, of course, spurious. Players who succumb to the bogus logic are rationalizing what they well know is illicit and immoral activity. Also, once a player is in a gangster's pocket, the criminal might be in a position to demand that the player deliberately lose a game and not just shave points.

Because of the potential for criminal involvement and the devastating effects this activity could have on the sports industry and young athletes' lives, many people desire to make betting on college basketball illegal in Nevada. They reason that making gambling illegal would reduce criminal activity. Actually, it could increase criminal activity, since many people would engage in illegal betting. Moreover, it is reckless to regulate for all because of the illegal behavior of some.

When I visited Lied Library at UNLV I left a card for Dr. David Schwartz, the director of the Center for Gaming Studies. Subsequently, Dr. Schwartz was good enough to let me interview him about a number of issues. One related to the arguments used by those who wish to abolish betting on college sports. Dr. Schwartz commented that the major argument used by proponents of such legislation related to the vulnerability of college athletes. He noted that all of the college gambling scandals to date involved illicit wagering, and none came as a result of shady undertakings by sports book managers who were operating legally. The beneficiaries and the perpetrators of the scandals were gangsters, not the backward-capped people reuniting with their college buddies who cram into sports books this weekend. Abolishing betting in Las Vegas would not stop criminals from approaching vulnerable athletes.

Foul!

In the high-rise seats at the top of the Imperial Palace amphitheater I sit next to two men who are betting the horses. It seems to me that they are losing continuously. After each defeat, they shake their heads and offer a postrace postmortem as they rip up their tickets.

"Yeah, well, that's what happens when you guard the rail."

"Can't win if you get boxed in."

"Jockey's gotta want to win."

They notice me listening. Instead of considering me to be an eavesdropper they share their sententious wisdom with me. One nods to me and explains, "If you wait too late to make your move, you wind up out of the money."

Theo and Rich are betting the horses as a sidebar to their basketball wagering. I ask if they come to March Madness often. Theo's straight-faced response—after what seems like a string of I don't know how many consecutive losses—is a sweeping motion of his arm to encompass the scene around us.

"Wouldn't miss this," he says without a hint of sarcasm.

Rich says they have been coming to Las Vegas each March for the last six years. Theo says it is seven, and the two of them squabble for a few moments.

I sit near Theo and Rich for two hours and not once do either of them win a horse or basketball bet.

• • •

The Butler supporters I met Thursday at the Paris must be thrilled by their team's second-round outing. The Bulldogs are a 6½-point underdog but nevertheless are defeating Maryland and will advance to the Sweet Sixteen. While Butler is advancing a second game provides another example of how March Madness in Las Vegas generates drama and excitement.

The Louisville Cardinals, a 2½-point underdog, are playing the Texas A&M Aggies. Louisville is losing by 1 point, 70–69, and has the ball with only 5 seconds left. Theo, Rich, and I have bet on Louisville to beat the spread. The only way we can lose is if Texas A&M gets the ball from Louisville and scores, since even if Louisville scores 3, we would still win on the spread. It looks good.

The problem is this: Rick Pitino, the coach for Louisville, and all of his players want to win the game. They are not content to lose 70–69 so that Theo, Rich, and I can go home winners. The Cardinals take a shot to try and go ahead with 5 seconds left.

They miss the shot. Texas A&M gets the rebound with only 2 seconds remaining. As soon as the ball is secured by the Texas A&M player, a short, squat man sitting in the front row vaults out of his seat as if bounding from a trampoline. As he soars he shrieks one word: "Foul!"

Immediately, as if responding to the demand, Louisville pounces on the player with the ball and commits a foul.

This is an intelligent decision for the Louisville players and fans—and the A&M bettors. It is a terrible decision for us Louisville bettors, because if A&M makes both free throws and Louisville fails to score, the final score will be 72–69, and we will lose on the 2½-point spread. Undoubtedly, the man who rocketed up from his seat screaming "Foul!" is betting on A&M.

The A&M player who was fouled walks calmly to the foul line. Theo mutters "Come on nine, come on nine, come on nine," temporarily distracted by yet another near-miss on the horse track. He receives more bad news when the A&M player makes both foul shots. The last-second heave by Louisville is unsuccessful, and they lose 72–69. The man sitting directly in front of me slaps his forehead like a cartoon character, another Louisville loser for sure. The leaping man in front is doing a little bouncing jig to the window to cash his slip.

Theo and Rich sigh.

"That's what happens when you don't know who to foul," says Rich.

"That's what happens when you're a six seed," says Theo.

"That's why it pays to lay the lumber," nods Rich.

Theo pokes Rich in the ribs. He points to the most recent losing horse race. "Looka here."

Rich takes a look and snorts. "That's what happens when you draw the nine pole."

A woman, a rarity here, has moved to a spot to my left. She makes an entry into a loose-leaf notebook.

"Go Aggies," she mutters.

"You rooting for A&M?" I ask.

"I am today," she says.

Feeling Lucky

The sad sack team of Theo and Rich are depressing. I need to take a walk. I leave the Imperial Palace and head up the Strip toward the Venetian. Despite the atypically hot weather, the Strip is mobbed at 2:45 this Saturday afternoon. Many bettors walk from one casino to another, holding the omnipresent betting slips and discussing strategy with their mates. I flag down the Arkansas crew from the Venetian and begin to ask them about the Louisville game. One puts up his hand like a traffic cup. "Do not talk to me about the Louisville game," he says. I wave to the California contingent I met in Bally's on Wednesday night huddled by a stoplight. "How you doing?" one shouts at me. I give them a thumbs up. One of the trio is lugging a twelve-pack.

It is St. Patty's day so even more drunk people are out on the Strip than usual. Here, and maybe elsewhere, St. Patty's Day just seems like another excuse to drink. Maybe Las Vegas provides a license for boozing that requires no rationalizations. Even in the afternoon the bars are mobbed. Outside the bars, nearly one in four pedestrians is holding a plastic cup filled with something that will knock you out if you consume enough of it. Too many men and women look as if they have done just that.

A thirty-something woman is clad completely in green, to the extent that she is clad at all. She is a very large woman and she is bombed. Her low-cut top has two words scrawled along the area of her navel: "Feeling Lucky?" On the back it reads, "Treesome." Three trees are intertwined below the written message. A red-faced slobbering man stumbles along laughing hysterically. His two slightly less drunk buddies prop him up. The drunk man's T-shirt reads, "You Looked Better on MySpace." I wonder if a woman gave him this shirt after an initial date.

Take the Money and Runnnn

I have it figured out now. I like three parlays and feel very good about them all. These bets will be winners. I am into it now. I am one of the boys.

The scene in the Venetian this Saturday is even wilder than it was on Thursday. A thousand rowdy men, each holding a beer bottle, spew basketball wisdom. Bettors line the walls of the sports book in such thick clusters that hardly any aisle space is left for the cocktail waitresses to squeeze through. The place is so boisterous that it looks like something created by Hollywood. Waitresses carry twenty to thirty bottles of beer on a tray, bettors scream crazily for their bets, a woman wearing little more than a tray around her waist coos "Cigars, cigarettes," security guards look out for who knows what, and bettors stream endlessly in looking for a place to sit. It is a madhouse.

I get on the queue to place my three can't miss parlays. A fellow in the front row who must have camped out to get his spot sits cross-legged on the carpet with a box of Krispy Kreme donuts, a pizza, and a six-pack.

"The three main food groups?" I ask.

He snorts and shrugs.

"All you need is a whore," suggests someone else.

"Maybe later," he says.

On the line someone is cursing about the Ohio State game. I grew up in Brooklyn and have watched the Sopranos. I have listened to crude barflies in taverns late at night. Nevertheless, I am shaking my head at the number of F-bombs exploding behind me.

"That fucking ref should be fucking shot for not fucking calling that fucking intentional on fucking Oden."

Pick a noun, any noun. Regardless of the noun the adjective was always the same. After informing all that he liked "the fucking chicken ala king" but did not like the "fucking peach pie" at the "fucking buffet" he says that he "isn't standing on this fucking line anymore." Nobody begs him to stay.

A fellow in front of me is moaning about his terrible luck.

"You want a winner?" he says to me. "Do just the opposite of what I do." This may be the fourth time this weekend someone has made this recommendation to me. And always the person with this advice is either considering making a bet or on line waiting to place one. This moaner, for example, is about to put $100 down on Pitt.

"Pitt's a gimme," he wheezes. "They gotta cover. vcu cannot stay with Pitt. The Duke game was a fluke. But, hey, listen to me. I haven't won squat."

Out of nowhere another fellow swings by to shmooze with us. He says, "Okay fellas, what do you want to know?" Then he regales us with his wisdom. In the three days I have been here other people just like this guy have surfaced from nowhere to offer intelligence without any sort of provocation. This particular individual tells those in the vicinity that he is a North Carolina season ticket holder. He guarantees that the Tarheels will cover the spread against Michigan State later today.

"Ten and a half?" asks a very tall man on the queue. He is referring to the lumber North Carolina will have to cover for a successful wager.

"Ten and a half, big fella," asserts the pundit. "I have seen every Tarheel game this year. Plus, the Big Ten sucks."

"I don't know. Ten a half?"

"Ten and a half," affirms the expert. "Will do."

"Hey, hustle it up!" yells someone from the back of the queue.

No one is permitted to place a bet after a game has begun, so bettors get anxious if a game is minutes from starting and the line is moving slowly. It's a remarkable sight when people who have been waiting on line to place a bet get shut out because the game has started. Furious men slap hundred dollar bills against their palms and explode volcanically because they have been deprived of the chance to throw their money away. Yesterday at the Imperial Palace right before a tip-off I was nearly knocked over by a heavy fellow bounding off the escalator, hoping to have a shot at squandering his savings.

For the casino owners, this is a wonderful business. Customers anxiously wait in line, aching for a chance to give their money away. Few of the customers will receive anything at all in exchange. Yet they return hour after hour and get upset when they are unable to give their money away.

And now, apparently, I am one of them.

"Hey, hustle it up," I say. "Put a move on. Place your bets and get out of there."

I ask the expert about my three parlays. The linchpin for each of the bets is Pitt. I think that game is a lock. Pitt has to beat Virginia Commonwealth by 6½.

The expert weighs in.

"You cannot, I repeat, you cannot, lose betting Pitt against VCU. I repeat. You cannot lose betting on Pitt."

"Can't miss?" I ask. I catch myself speaking and thinking like all those folks around me who are scribbling notes on betting slips and in loose-leaf folders.

"Cannot miss. VCU played its heart out to beat Duke. I have season tickets to North Carolina," he reminds me. "I see Duke all the friggin' time. VCU had to leave its nuts on the court to beat Duke."

"You think they'll have nothing left."

"VCU has nothing left, my friend. ZEE ROW. Pitt will eat them up and spit them out. You want to know why?"

I don't ask because I know he is going to tell me anyway.

"Pitt is a powerhouse in the Big East. They demolished Wright State on Thursday by twenty-one points. A three seed. A three. VCU plays in the Colonial. What is the Colonial? The Colonial. Hah. James Madison University plays in the Colonial! James Madison. Give me a break. VCU is an eleven seed. Eleven."

"They're only laying six and a half. If Pitt is so good why are they only laying six and a half?"

"Here's what. You want to know what? Here's what. People saw VCU beat Duke. All of a sudden VCU is the cat's pajamas. They bet VCU." He punches me on the shoulder. "You know what happens when the money comes in on VCU?"

"The spread goes down."

"It goes downnnnnn." he says as he takes a finger, raises it toward his chin, points it toward the floor, and then moves the finger south while making a fizzling sound with his mouth. "Wayyy downnnnn. Pitt will win by a dozen. Lay the lumber, take the money, and run." He points his finger straight ahead and moves it way to the right. "Lay the lumber, take the money, and runnnnnn."

Somehow I feel less assured after listening to this wizard. Nevertheless, when I get to the window I bet my three parlays with Pitt as the linchpin. My three parlays are Pitt minus 6½, BC–Georgetown under 126½, Washington State–Vanderbilt over 129; Pitt minus 6½, Indiana plus 8, North Carolina minus 10½; and Pitt minus 6½, Georgetown minus 6½, and UCLA–Indiana under 127.

Take the money and runnnnnnn.

I am lucky to grab a seat at the bar. A vacant barstool beside me has a piece of lined paper resting on it that reads "Reserved." Shortly after I sit down, a well-lubricated man of about thirty-five pokes me and asks if the guy who was sitting in this seat was a big or a little man. I tell him that I haven't seen anyone sitting there. The inebriated fellow parks himself on the stool and says he is betting on a small man. He begins to play a computer poker game embedded in the bar top. While doing so he spews a monologue that is difficult to decode. He seems to have lost a bunch on Wisconsin yesterday because the phrase "Friggin' Cheeseheads" punctuates his comments with astonishing frequency. When a waitress walks by, the muttering poker player stops rambling, elbows me in the ribs, and opines, "That is a pair of tits there, my friend."

Two minutes later he rears his head back. "I want you to know," he says, apropos of nothing, "that I happen to be kicking the shit out of this poker machine."

The man sitting to my other side is a different character altogether. A very serious-looking fellow, he's also betting the horses while holding a stack of basketball bets. In front of him are racing sheets and basketball information. He has a notebook, but as opposed to others I have seen over this weekend, his is a plain spiral pad that appears to be just a place where he records bets and outcomes during the weekend. In his right hand he has a pencil;

in his left, the betting tickets and a wad of bills. Occasionally he removes some bills to place a wager, folds the remaining ones, and places the stack in the breast pocket of his shirt.

Roger is not chatty but is amiable. While occasionally he raises his penciled hand to indicate that he can't talk because of an ongoing horse race or some other topic of contemplation, he is otherwise willing to discuss his betting strategy. Roger knows what he is doing as well as a bettor can.

I ask him if he comes each year for March Madness and he nods. "Missed a couple years in the late nineties. Didn't come out in two thousand and two after Nine-Eleven—didn't want to fly," he adds with a sheepish smile. "But yeah, pretty much I've been here every year since the tournament went to sixty-four."

Roger is about fifty. He is from the borough of Queens in New York. He works in Manhattan as a lawyer for the City.

"It's a job. Not corporate pay, but it's okay. I'm single."

I tell him about my parlays and he nods politely. Unlike the wizard, I get the sense that Roger does not think much of the bets, but he tells me that he will be pulling for me. Without criticizing my wagers explicitly, he suggests that a way to make some money is to bet a money line parlay wagering on underdogs.

"Of course, you are going to lose more than you're going to win, but if you connect the payday is very good."

I want to know how it works.

"Okay. Let's take the games played already today. Let's say you bet Xavier, Butler, and Louisville—three dogs in a money line parlay. Well, you are a loser because Xavier and Louisville lost, but not by a whole lot. Xavier wins that game if Oden gets an intentional foul, and how he does not get an intentional foul is shake your head stuff, you know what I mean?

"So Xavier almost wins. Butler *does* win. Louisville has a chance to win with seconds left and the ball. Three dogs come very close to winning. That is a helluva payday if it comes in on a fifty-dollar bet."

He shrugs. "So, if you can find three dogs in the tournament that you like, bet a money line parlay on them, and if you score you can lose a good many games and races and return home a winner. 'Course," he adds self-effacingly, "it's Saturday and so far I haven't hit one yet, but I have one riding now."

"Who?"

"I had Butler earlier today. I need vcu and Vanderbilt now. Two Vs." He flashes me a gap-toothed grin while making the V for victory sign with his fingers. "Two Vs," he says again.

"You like vcu to win against Pitt?" Roger sounds like he knows what he is doing and I have Pitt as a gimme, the key to my payday.

"Look," he says. "It's a long shot. Most people like Pitt. You've got some good bets there. You laying seven with Georgetown?"

"No, six and a half."

"Hmm. Very good. You'll cover."

● ● ●

After listening to Roger I remember that once a few years back I was at a window collecting what I thought was a $60 killing on a parlay bet. I saw a crowd gathering at a nearby station and two or three Brinks-truck types attending to someone. Joining the crowd, I saw that two young men were picking up $35,000 they had won on a parlay. The Brinks officers carefully counted out the money. I did not ask what kind of parlay it was that brought in this bonanza, but I know—at least from this firsthand observation—that while it is highly unlikely, it is not impossible to make a good deal of money betting on the games.

This afternoon can make Roger $1,000 wealthier, yet you

would not know it from his demeanor for nearly all of the contests. As opposed to the maniac sitting to my right, Roger is soberly watching the games, alternately checking out his horse bets and scribbling in his spiral notebook.

Three college kids are walking through the space in front of Roger and me. They pass us and halt a few steps beyond the drunk playing poker at the bar. They are chatting excitedly, and I gather this is their first trip to Vegas for March Madness. They are gushing as they check out the scene. One of them takes out a cell phone and in an attempt to capture the wildness takes a photo of the masses in the sports book.

"Uh-oh," Roger mutters.

Within a minute, maybe fifteen seconds, security guards surround the students. The guards begin to admonish the now visibly nervous young men. Cell phones and cameras are strictly prohibited in a sports book. I was not aware of the rule, but Roger was. The students certainly were not. After a short but intense confrontation during which it becomes obvious that the three were tourists and not about to use the photo or their cell phones to gain any advantage, the guards disperse. The students look like their lives have just been saved as they bolt from the sports book.

"Very big no-no," Roger says soberly.

"Some shit just went down there, buddy boy," says the poker player even though he had not taken his eyes off the embedded machine during the course of the commotion.

●●●

As the two V contests progress, it appears as if Roger will not make his payday, but I may well make mine. Washington State leads at halftime by 8 over his first V, Vanderbilt. The Virginia Commonwealth game with Pittsburgh, which began about ten minutes later, is still in the first half, but that one is not even close. Just as the wizard and, apparently, three-quarters of the bettors in the Venetian figured, Pittsburgh is shellacking Roger's second V. This is good news for me, but I sort of feel bad for Roger, for whom I've developed an affinity.

Vanderbilt finally gives Roger some hope. In the second half they come back strongly to tie the game at 60 and have possession of the ball with 24 seconds remaining. Both teams miss shots in the last seconds and the contest heads into overtime.

"Still alive," Roger says evenly.

The overtime is similarly tense, but Roger may have one of the Vs necessary for his $1,000 payday. Vanderbilt leads 69–66 with 51 seconds remaining. Washington State, however, counters with a 3-point field goal and ties the score at 69. Vanderbilt calls a time-out with 8 seconds left and tries to design a play that will result in a victory. The crowd at the Venetian is chanting "defense" as Vanderbilt begins its possession, reflecting a Washington State sentiment in the house.

"I guess you don't want defense," I say to Roger.

"No, I do not," he says, and for the first time I see some emotion on his face.

The drunk to my right for no apparent reason feels it is high time for him to mutter his favorite phrase: "Friggin' Cheeseheads."

Unfortunately for Roger, the "defense" chant has an effect. Vanderbilt loses possession of the ball, but the team maintains enough composure to thwart a last-second attempt by Washington State. The game goes into a second overtime.

"Close," I say.

"Too close. Dodged a bullet. Probably doesn't matter, though," Roger says as he points to the television that is showing the Virginia Commonwealth–Pittsburgh game.

Roger needs vcu to win, and now, with 12 minutes remaining in the second half, his second V is down by 19 points. Roger seems like one of the more decent people I have met in these days so I feel for him and his impending loss. Even though he seems like a bright man, I truly do not know how he could have thought that vcu could play with Pittsburgh. I am sitting pretty with the Pitt lock; the under with Boston College is already a winner; Georgetown covered the 6½ over bc, 62–55; and the 129 over in the Vanderbilt game is well over because of the double overtime. I am going to do well with my parlays. But I feel for Roger.

In the second overtime, Vanderbilt goes ahead 76–74 with 28 seconds remaining. It seems that the lead will increase, because a Vanderbilt player is on the foul line for two free throws that could swell the lead to 4, making Roger almost certainly a winner. Uncharacteristically, Roger slams his hand onto the table sending pencils and a Styrofoam coffee cup flying when after clanking the first shot, the Vanderbilt player goes on to miss the second one as well.

"Damn," he says.

Washington State hoists a 3-point attempt with 17 seconds left but does not connect. When Vanderbilt secures the rebound, Roger exhales and looks at me. The first V has won in double overtime.

"One V down," he says.

"Yeah," I say. "Congratulations. What a great game. Sorry about the second V."

He points to a screen.

I had stopped paying attention to the Pitt game when the gap was 19. Roger had not. I cannot believe the score when I look at the television. Pitt apparently has collapsed. The second V and Pitt are tied with seconds left to go. The game will almost definitely go into overtime to break the tie. So much for the wizard and all the other pundits on the queue who predicted an easy victory for Pitt.

"One V to go," Roger says. "I think vcu may be able to do it in overtime."

I am happier for Roger than I am unhappy for me. Pitt is my gimmee and my linchpin, but Roger stands to win $1,000 if vcu can win this game in overtime.

But the Pitt game, as it turns out, may not go into overtime. With only 2 seconds remaining in the tied contest a Pittsburgh player named Levance Fields has been fouled. Fields is a regular for Pittsburgh. He will have an opportunity to shoot two free throws with 2 seconds left. Roger's bid for a $1,000 payday looks lost.

Again, an otherwise and typically calm Roger slams the table ferociously, sending papers flying. When Fields is fouled, "For the love of Jesus, God damn it," comes rumbling from somewhere near Roger's belly. He walks around his seat in a circle. He picks up one of the papers that had dropped to the floor and balls it up. In frustration, he winds up and throws the crumpled sphere like a right fielder trying to peg out a player tagging up from third base. He mutters something and sits down despondently.

Roger, of course, hopes the Pitt player misses both shots. Nearly everyone in this packed madhouse also wants Fields to miss both shots even though most in here are cheering for Pittsburgh. If you have Pitt minus 6½ or vcu on the money line, overtime is your only hope. If Fields connects on even one of his shots, there will be no overtime, and Pitt will win by 2 but not cover the 6½ points. Then not only will Roger and I lose, but an army of beer-quaffing very-close-to-miserable bettors will lose as well.

As the Pittsburgh player goes to the free throw line, the din from the crowd in this Las Vegas casino trying to razz the player taking a shot in Buffalo is overwhelming.

"Choke, you sonofabitch!" screams a man seated nearby who looks as sedate as a small-town fifth grade teacher.

But what are the chances—even with the psychic energy and plaintive exhortations intended to discourage Pittsburgh's Levance Fields—that a starter for a Big East team is going to miss two free shots that can win a game with 2 seconds left?

He misses both shots.

A roar comes up in the Venetian like I have not heard since I was in the Imperial Palace two hours earlier and Ohio State hit a 3 to send its game into overtime.

Inexplicably, the knuckleheaded poker player mutters "Friggin' Cheeseheads."

One poor shmo standing in front of us has VCU plus 6½ points. He would have been a winner had Levance Fields hit even one of these free throws. When the second one clanks away he wheels around and squawks.

"Oh fixaroonee! Fixaroonee! Some serious point shaving shit going down there. Tell me that is not a fixaroonee! Clanking two foul shots like that. Fixaroonee! Fixaroonee!"

The overtime is excruciating for Roger and everybody else in the sports book. People looked like they were wiped after the Washington State–Vanderbilt double overtime, so for this game, one might think that the bettors would have little left. But the cheering is furious and wild.

"Let's go Pittsburgh, let's go!" is chanted rhythmically in the casino.

The cheering does no good for the masses. Pittsburgh manages to win, but not by enough. The only happy people in the Venetian are my fixaroonee-squawking neighbor and those who betted along with him.

I look at Roger. "Sorry," I say.

He smiles wanly and shrugs, "Hey, I gave it a good shot."

The final is 84–79. Pitt minus 6½ was a lock for three-fourths of the Venetian, including me, but we are losers by 1 measly point. I take a walk through the sports book to look for the wizard. I can't find him, but I hear the words "Fucking Pitt" wherever I go. The pizza-and-donut-eating, whore-considering, six-pack-guzzling man is still sitting with legs crossed in the front of the Venetian. He is shaking his head saying "Fucking Pitt" like a mantra.

All three of my parlays are shot. Every single one of my bets is a winner except for the Pitt game. I am amused by the scene but consider joining the F-bombing multitude complaining about Pittsburgh.

An elderly couple from England wanders by and can't get over the collective gloom.

"Why are so many people disappointed in Pittsburgh? Your team won."

I try to explain the distress, telling them that the spread is 6½. They cannot get it but are amused nonetheless.

In the middle of all this tumult a bride walks with her wedding party along a concourse just beyond the sports book. She is crying tears of joy, and her attendants are similarly swelled with happiness at their friend's celebration as they march behind her in matching attire. They walk past the roulette wheel, craps tables, and blackjack area apparently oblivious to what is going on. They might as well be in a church. But they are not in a church. No church I know of employs a chant of "Fucking Pitt." Yet the bride and her friends are promenading through as if blissfully unaware of the gloom and chaos around them.

I point out the sight to Roger.

Unmoved, he says, "Maybe they're crying because they had Pitt."

An enormous amount of beer has been consumed at the Venetian. Consequently the walkway to the restroom is well traveled, and the sights along that concourse are something to see. One fellow is on the phone, apparently to his wife. She seems not to be able to understand why he has gone to Las Vegas to reduce their savings.

"Well," he says, "if that is all that you have to say to me, if that's all you have to say, then I'm just going to have to say good-bye."

Half a dozen bettors lean along the concourse wall, scouring their betting sheets.

A heavy man emerges from the bathroom just as I am about to enter. He adjusts his pants, shakes his head, and mutters to me, "There's always surprises."

I find an open urinal, take my spot, and witness a classic scene. A man standing next to me is studying a betting sheet that he has propped up with his left hand while he is guiding his fluid with his right. A cigar is clamped tightly between his teeth. He finishes his business, flushes with his right hand, and wheels to leave. He sees me looking at him.

"Fucking Pitt," he says as he replaces the cigar, zips up his fly, and exits.

●●●

I swing by the bar to say goodbye to Roger. He waves but is busy reviewing what looks to be tomorrow's horse racing sheets. The "Cheesehead" fellow is gone, as is "Fixaroonee."

I leave the sports book and walk through the blackjack area. A fellow who looks to be every bit of seventy-five stands by the tables moaning about his fortune to nobody in particular. When he catches me looking at him, he approaches like a panhandler who has identified a sympathetic prospect. "I bet two dogs and two favorites and I can't get a freaking break. Last night I was up a thousand dollars." I shrug my shoulders.

Out of the Venetian and onto the Strip I see a man with a T-shirt that says what I was thinking about Pitt hours ago: "Sure Thing."

Rub Me for Luck

I walk to Bally's to watch the last two games of the day. The Strip is still busy. A line of people fight to get onto a packed bus that stops outside of Harrah's. Banging into this queue are packs of revelers almost all of whom are hauling booze in some container or other as they jostle and push their way from one party scene to the next. The sidewalk has no space for maneuvering.

A few doors down from Harrah's, O'Shea's is engaged in yet another of its twenty-four consecutive happy hours. The dwarf dressed up as a leprechaun is still barking, encouraging revelers to come in and consume. Many revelers, whether because of the leprechaun's persuasion or for some other reason, seem inclined to do just that. Outside the Flamingo a tavern has a balcony over which soused customers hold enormous plastic containers filled with powerful-looking concoctions. Couples walking north away from the Paris drink from even larger containers shaped like the Eiffel Tower. The amount of booze people are knocking back is stunning. It is only about 5 in the afternoon and yet people sit on the sidewalk sleeping or passed out from having consumed too much.

Many varieties of green hats bob in the crowd around me. T-shirts celebrating the Irish are worn by people representing several demographic categories. Everyone appears to be Irish or at least celebrating the day as if they are.

A couple walks toward me, and like so many others, they are jovial and are holding the required beverages in plastic cups. His right arm is draped on her shoulders, and her left is around his waist. He wraps his right arm around her body so he can fondle her exposed belly. She is giggling. "Stop it," she laughs while squirming, although the two of them appear to be having a good time. She's probably in her early twenties; he may be a few years older. As they walk past me, he removes his hand from her belly and grasps as much of her bottom as he can.

"Oooh," she giggles. "Stop it."

He does, but after a swig of brew they turn to each other for a smooch. As they walk away I see the writing on the back of his T-shirt: "Four leaf clover. Rub me for luck."

The crowd at Bally's seems exhausted. This makes sense. The two games that will conclude the day will be the thirty-ninth and fortieth of the weekend. Indiana will be playing UCLA and Michigan State will contend with North Carolina.

My three parlays are history because of the Pitt collapse, but I still have the under on Indiana–UCLA that had been recommended by my doctor friend this morning. I also made a bet based on the wisdom of the wizard who recommended North Carolina against Michigan State regardless of the 10½ points of lumber I had to lay.

I find a seat in the last row of the sports book amphitheater beside a lean, tall, balding man. He holds a beer in his hand, and a bucket with three empty bottles sits on the table in front of him. Don tells me he is a retired marketing professor who worked at North Dakota State. Originally from New York, he now lives in San Diego and is here—as he has been each year for the last decade—to watch the games and the scene. Typically, he tells me, he attends with a professor friend who works at Western Michigan. The two academics met at a conference and have written papers together on sports marketing. His buddy, unfortunately, could not make it this year. So Don drove up from San Diego alone and is staying this year at a cheap hotel on the outskirts of town.

"If Teddy was here we'd stay closer and sleep around here. But alone? Why spend the extra money to sleep on the Strip? The parking lots are free. I drive up at eight in the morning, park in a lot, watch basketball all day long, and then drive back to crash." He takes a swig of his beer.

"Only problem is this." He lifts and wags the bottle. "You drink enough of these, you should not drive back to any motel."

He stares for a second at the beer bottle and emits a chuckle.

"I can tell you a funny story about how beer actually helped me win once."

I ask him to go ahead.

"Nah, never mind. I'm talking too much. You'll think I'm bragging."

"Go ahead."

"Alright. You sure?"

"Sure. I want to hear it."

"This is wild and I had nothing to do with it. I take no credit. Sheer luck. Sure I'm not talking too much?"

"Go ahead," I say again.

He tells me that he had been drinking one night and put down some money on a game to be played on the next day. He bet on a team to win laying 9½ points. He can't even remember now, at this telling, who was playing whom. The next morning he woke up with a hangover and forgot that he had bet on this particular game the night before. Now sober, he goes to a casino, bets the same game, but this time he bets the underdog, getting 10½ because the stupid money has affected the spread. So he has two bets, one for Team X laying 9½ and one for the opponent Team

Y getting 10½. When the game is over the final score is Team X 60–Team Y 50.

Ron laughs. "I win twice. I win the bet I made when I was hammered because I only had to give up nine and a half. I win the bet I made when I was sober because I got ten and a half." He laughs again.

"Believe me, if I tried to do that myself, sober, I would lose both bets, not win them both. My life should be so lucky." He pauses, starts to say something about his life, then thinks better of it. "Ah, never mind."

We talk some basketball. He assures me that I have nothing to worry about with my North Carolina game, concurring with the wizard. In his opinion, The Big Ten, except for Ohio State, is overrated and awful.

"The Big Ten sucks. Believe me. The team I like in the tournament is Florida."

"Florida?"

"Florida. Yes. They'll win. The talent is overwhelming. They haven't even been trying all year."

"What about Ohio State?" I ask.

He waves. "You see them almost lose to Xavier today?"

I nod.

"Should have lost. Ref had no courage. That was an intentional foul if there ever is such a thing as an intentional foul. Ohio State will not be able to play with Florida. You watch. The Big Ten sucks."

It turns out that I have been advised wisely during this portion of the tournament. My poker-playing doctor friend assured me that the 127 under in the UCLA game was a guarantee and he certainly seems wise. The two teams do not come close to 127 in their 54–49 game. The wizard and my new professor friend here at Bally's did not steer me wrong, either. Laying 10½ on North

Carolina is not a problem, as they defeat Michigan State by 14.

"Looks like you were right with North Carolina," I say to Don.

"The Big Ten Sucks. Indiana won with the spread, but they lost, too. You watch. Wisconsin and Purdue will be done after tomorrow also. The Big Ten sucks."

His concern for sobriety on his ride home does not preclude having two with me during the contests we watch.

I shake hands with Don as I leave Bally's. It is only 9 p.m. but I feel the need to get some sleep. I return to the Imperial Palace and take what has become a regular trip up to the sports book before I go to my room. A long line of bettors hugs the wall, waiting either to cash in on their winnings or make bets for Sunday. I look for the genius from Raleigh, but after Xavier lost on the money line he may have gone directly to the airport. I go up to my room and record some notes on my computer before I fall asleep.

● ● ●

I wake up at 1 a.m., lie in bed for forty minutes, and decide to see if Las Vegas is still happening at this time of the night.

There are two empty Corona bottles in the elevator. Down in the lobby at 1:53, the place is as raucous and lively as can possibly be. It seems no different now than it had been at 9. As I walk through the casino I see something that stops me short. The bride from this afternoon is throwing dice at the craps table with her bridesmaids cheering her on. Still in her gown, she is talking the talk. "C'mon eleven," she rasps. The groom is not around. Maybe he's at the blackjack table. Many of the onlookers are cheering for the bride, who hits a 7 then tries to make a mark of 10 before succumbing to snake eyes. The crowd applauds her anyway and wishes her good luck.

I leave the Imperial Palace and walk toward the Paris. I overhear the conversation of a young couple on the far side of sobriety.

"That's when the Indian bitch shoved me," says the man.

"Yeah," says the woman, "and that's when I fucking nailed her."

At 2:20 the poker room at the Paris is hopping. Outside the Paris a sleeping drunk sits like a statue holding a bottle of beer. Six guffawing twentysomethings stagger past without noticing him, well on their way to their own oblivion.

At the Bellagio three young kids sit in the sports book. They study betting sheets very soberly without paying any attention to me or each other. I sit in a chair and look at the near-empty facility that I know will be crammed in a few hours. As I get up to leave, one of the guys lifts his head.

"You like Wisconsin?" He asks.

I cannot resist.

"Nah," I say. "Friggin' Cheeseheads."

Hanging Out with Jesus

Despite the very late Saturday night I am up early on Sunday morning. I arrive at the Imperial Palace sports book at 6:45 and am not surprised to see two huddled groups of bettors up in the amphitheater discussing the day's wagers.

A lone man waits on the betting line for the windows to open at 8. Two others stand at the counter staring at the odds scrawled on the whiteboard behind it. They talk to each other as they gaze ahead at the lines for today's games.

"That over on the Tennessee game is way high."

"Mmm. Virginia can shoot, though."

"Way high."

"Virginia can shoot. You saw that guy hit the threes."

"Still. I like the under."

"Okay. The under, there. What about Wisconsin?"

It is appropriate that these words are among the first I hear this day. This now-familiar and predictable patter has pervaded each of my days in Las Vegas. On Thursday, I might have tried to wheedle my way into this conversation, or at least have hung around to hear more, but today I feel as if I could write the script for this exchange.

On the way out of the sports book I see a pamphlet entitled "When the Fun Stops" in the area where the betting sheets are laid out. The pamphlet is about problem gambling. It has been nearly buried by the betting sheets for basketball, hockey, spring training baseball, arena football, and NFL futures. One particular sheet that has found its way inside the pamphlet, like a bookmark, lists the over-under on Mariano Rivera saves, Curt Shilling strikeouts, Pedro Martinez wins, hits by Ichiro Suzuki, most home runs that will be hit by any player during the 2007 season, and most strikeouts by any pitcher during the 2007 season. "When the Fun Stops" targets those who might want to consider the possibility that they have a gambling problem if they're thinking of betting on Ichiro Suzuki at 6:50 on a Sunday morning before baseball season has even begun.

The American Psychiatric Association, in the fourth edition of *Diagnostic and Statistical Manual of Mental Disorders*, defines a pathological gambler as one who exhibits "persistent and recurrent maladaptive behavior that disrupts personal, family, or vocational pursuits." The APA lists several characteristics of such people. For example, they lie to family members or therapists to conceal their involvement in gambling; they commit illegal acts such as forgery, fraud, theft, or embezzlement to finance gambling; they become restless or irritable when attempting to cut down or stop gambling; they have jeopardized or lost a significant relationship or job because of gambling; they need to gamble with increasing amounts of money in order to achieve the desired excitement; or they rely on others to provide money to relieve a desperate financial situation caused by gambling.

I would not be surprised to discover that some of people with whom I have interacted here are problem gamblers. However, it seems that the majority of these bettors do not fit this profile at all. Most of them are college students, recent graduates, or professionals who are spending disposable income on a vacation. I wonder if people who truly have a gambling problem would even consider that possibility when they come across a booklet like "When the Fun Stops."

•••

A cluster of Wisconsin fans adorned with matching Grateful Red T-shirts are buzzing near the buffet line across from the ballroom. Not one of this group looks to be younger than forty-five. The alumni have united this weekend to cheer for their alma mater. The Emperor's Buffet opens at 7. In a few minutes the Grateful Red will attack the bacon, eggs, pancakes, and everything else at the buffet, but the energy that fuels their voracity will at least in part be due to March Madness excitement. The Badgers play an 11:45 second-round game against the University of Las Vegas at Nevada. In the vernacular of the fan, these guys are pumped, and their energy is contagious.

"You like your chances?" I ask one.

"We'll see. Wait and see," says a cautious man with three days' worth of gray beard.

"You think you'll cover?"

"Never bet the spread with the Badgers. Never bet on the Badgers. Too nervous."

Aside from the jumpy Grateful Red, the activity outside the viewing ballroom on this Sunday is not nearly as frenetic as it has been at the same time on Thursday, Friday, or Saturday. Some folks appear to have made an early exit or are just too tired at this point to gear up so early. I ride the escalator down to the main floor of the casino and overhear a few sleepy hoop bettors talking on their way up. One young fellow says to his two friends "You know, I think three days of this is plenty." This observation, however, does not seem to deter any among the trio from proceeding to the sports book on this fourth day.

On the main floor of the casino I pass one of the bars. It is 6:55. A man sits at the bar drinking a Heineken and looking at a betting sheet. He has a pencil behind one ear. I figure it is best not to approach him: his T-shirt reads, "My Anger Management Class Pisses Me Off."

• • •

I leave the Imperial Palace and turn south toward the Flamingo. Again I pass O'Shea's and see that they were not prevaricating when they advertised a 24–7 happy hour. On this Sunday morning, customers take advantage of the hotel's alleged largesse. A flashing neon billboard high above the casino invites customers to "Check out our slots. We're practically giving it away."

At Flamingo Road I decide to cross the Strip. On the pedestrian overpass a couple approaches me. They are walking unsteadily and each is holding the omnipresent plastic cup. The woman looks to be in her mid-twenties, and the young man, a few steps behind her, may be a few years her senior. The woman staggers up to me. She is really looped.

"Congratulate us!" she says. "We just decided to get married. We did it. Congratulate us. We did it."

Her newlywed groom is so far gone he can barely string sentences together. Nevertheless, he makes an attempt. "Look at her. Isn't she gorgeous? Aren't I one lucky sonofabitch? I mean. Really. Congratulate me."

"No, honey. Congratulate *us*. Congratulate *us*."

"Yeah. Congratulate *us*."

I congratulate them.

They hoist their plastic cups and ask me to make a toast. I make a toast. They knock plastic cups and knock down most of what is left in the containers.

"We're married." She says after she's swallowed. "Holy fucking shit. We're married. Oh excuse me." She covers her mouth. "Sorry for the language. But I mean, holy fucking shit, we're married." She starts giggling.

"Isn't she gorgeous?" The groom says again.

She is a looker, at least to my eyes, even if this is not her best moment.

"She sure is." I say as I try to wave goodbye.

"Hey take a picture, mister. Please."

She holds out her cell phone and shows me how to aim and shoot. I photograph the newlyweds, return the phone, and walk toward the Bellagio.

"Thank you!" they scream after me. The thought comes to my mind that it's a lock that they will be divorced almost as soon as they sober up.

I cross the pedestrian overpass, descend to street level, and stand near the artificial lake that fronts the Bellagio. This is a beautiful sight at any time and particularly attractive on a relatively quiet Sunday morning. At regular intervals, water bursts from pipes buried in the lake, creating fountains that magically sway to the rhythm of music boomed out to the Strip. Pedestrians at all hours stop and enjoy the spectacle of this truly magnificently coordinated show. At this moment the fountains are not functioning, but Frank Sinatra is crooning over the speakers. One fellow, all by himself, is slow dancing to the music.

A van drives up to the hotel entrance. The driver parks near the water and emerges in a wet suit and snorkeling gear. Apparently he is a repairman of some sort. He waddles out into the artificial pond. Before submerging, he sings out the last words of "My Way" along with Frank.

I continue along the Strip up toward the Monte Carlo, New York New York, and Excalibur. A man wearing a Grateful Red T-shirt passes me and I say, "Go Badgers!" He responds in kind and pumps his fist in the air. Like his brethren at the Imperial Palace, he appears to be antsy for the game that will begin in four hours.

The Monte Carlo is a posh hotel, with an elegant bar area and gaming tables that seem to be populated by wealthy customers even this early in the morning. At an expensive-looking lounge next to the sports book a man still attired, it seems, for the prior night's show is wooing a similarly garbed woman with tales of his gambling exploits. He had a string of successes at the craps tables, but settled down to really score at a $100 blackjack table. I cannot tell if the woman really believes him or if he believes his story himself, but the two are making googly eyes at each other as he relays his tale of gaming conquests.

I cross back over the Strip at Tropicana Avenue and enter the Aladdin. The Aladdin is undergoing extensive renovations for the second time in a few years. I imagine that the scaffolding on the outside of the building must discourage some potential customers from entering. This is too bad for both the Aladdin and, at least, the sports bettors. The temporary sports book viewing area is excellent, with enormous TV screens and ample seating for as many bettors as might wish to attend. Two men in the know have already secured their seats in the sports book. Each has an outsized coffee, the extra-large you feel you need at 7:30 a.m. after you have watched forty basketball games while drinking beer incessantly for three days and staying up until 3 in the morning.

For the sake of research I force myself to walk up to them.

"Who do you like?"

I can tell that they are not eager to break their concentration by speaking with me. One fellow eventually picks up his head up and says, "Winthrop."

"Winthrop?"

"Bet the over with Winthrop and run."

The other man does not pick his head up but offers an opinion.

"There never was a gimmee like Memphis is a gimmee today."

I ask whether he bet on Pittsburgh yesterday.

He picks his head up for the first time.

"Do not talk to me about Pittsburgh."

I do not say a word.

"Do not talk to me about Pittsburgh."

I do not say a word.

"Just do not talk to me about Pittsburgh."

I emerge from the Aladdin and spot a down-and-out fellow seated in a stupor on top of a jersey barrier facing the Aladdin construction. Two beer bottles—one half empty—are by his side. Just beyond him an enormously busty woman hangs onto the arm of a relatively conservative-looking man. They are crossing the Strip near where the old Holiday Inn casino called the Boardwalk used to be. The Boardwalk and a series of small souvenir shops were destroyed during the last year to make way for construction of a new casino. This is a regular occurrence on the Strip: imploding older casinos to make way for more-modern hotels.

As this woman gets closer I see that she is wearing a tight-fitting top that is extraordinarily revealing. The words across her chest read, "Hang out with Jesus." As she and her companion walk away from me toward Tropicana Avenue, I read the back of her shirt: "He Hung Out with You."

On my way to the Imperial Palace, I turn around to take another look at the woman. A jogger running toward me approaches her, takes a long look, dodges her with some difficulty, turns around to take another look at her, then pulls up to me at a stop light. He jogs in place waiting for the light to change.

"You see who Jesus is hanging out with?" he asks me.

"I did."

He shakes his head. "Mom wanted me to spend more time with Jesus."

I ask if it is difficult to run along the Strip. He nods strongly in the affirmative as he continues to jog up and down.

"They sold everybody out building the hotels right to the curb. It's ridiculous. Lights take forever."

"Are there other places to run?"

"Sure. But it is the same everywhere around here. It's ridiculous."

The light changes and as he bolts out from the sidewalk he shouts, "Take care." Halfway across the intersection he turns around and, at significant peril, jogs a few steps back away from me. "Hang out with Jesus!" he yells before turning and jogging off.

The group of us crossing the street includes two pals studying betting sheets and discussing the downside of a wager they have made.

"But their backcourt might get into foul trouble," one says to the other.

"Look, we gotta be optimistic," his friend responds.

Their focus on the betting sheets makes me wonder if these two will barge into someone coming the other way, but they seem to effortlessly avoid collisions by swaying this way or that.

"They have no big man."

"You gotta be optimistic, Seth."

"I don't fucking know."

Seth is wearing a T-shirt that reads, "Trust Me. I'm a Doctor."

•••

Back at the Imperial Palace, the main floor is not what it was at 9 last night, but there is activity at the blackjack and craps tables, and many customers sit on stools in front of the one-armed bandits. Even though most of the slot players lose most of the time, none would agree that the casino is "giving it away."

A large crowd waits to get on the elevator. After my Felliniesque morning stroll, I need a cup of coffee to get back on track. That means another trip, like yesterday, to the Starbucks at Harrah's. If I can manage to avoid the blackjack tables, the coffee will cost me less than $72.50.

On the pedestrian bridge that connects the Imperial Palace to Harrah's, a young couple walking arm and arm emerges from the monorail stop. She looks to be in her late twenties, and he is a few years older. She has a pleased look on her face, and he is positively beaming. Both are neatly dressed, the man in a pair of khaki slacks and a black buttoned-down short-sleeved shirt, and the woman in well-ironed olive shorts and a black top. Her top has a collar and fits snugly. A Nike swoosh is visible just below her right shoulder, and a variation of the familiar Nike slogan is written across her chest. They spot me staring and smile mischievously as they pass. I get a better look at the announcement below the Nike swoosh.

"Just Did It," it reads.

I Bleed Scarlet

I finish my tall coffee and proceed to Harrah's temporary sports book. Some fifteen bettors wait to place a wager on today's games. The earliest contest begins almost an hour from now, a 9 a.m. tip-off between Tennessee and Virginia. Unlike yesterday, I get in line immediately. Not only will I be able to wager on the game, I can also avoid the blackjack tables. I rationalize that my basketball betting this morning will actually be a cost-cutting measure.

In the slow-moving line I have time to talk with a backward-capped kid in front of me. He wants to know my feelings on the Tennessee–Virginia game. I tell him that I am hardly an expert.

"Who is?" he snorts. "But, hey, who do you like?"

"I like Tennessee. Tennessee is only laying two and a half. They scored easily in their initial game."

"You like Tennessee, eh?"

"Yes. Tennessee. Virginia played a weak opponent in the first round and shot the lights out. I doubt they can shoot at such a high percentage again."

When I hear myself speaking I feel ridiculous. I sound as if I really know what I am talking about—and I do not. I sound just like the people I have been listening to this weekend who also sound like they know what they are talking about and also do not. Nobody betting the games against the spread could possibly know what they are talking about, since the spread makes each contest essentially a toss of the coin. A bettor against the spread might as well pick winners by making a snap decision ten seconds before placing his bet, or by chanting "Eenie, meenie, miney, moe."

"You like Tennessee, eh?" he asks again.

"Yeah, but don't listen to me."

"No. I think that makes sense. What about Memphis?"

I tell him someone at the Aladdin said Memphis minus 5½ is a lock.

"Everybody here has got a lock," he says. "And nobody here has a lock."

This is the most accurate piece of wisdom I have heard in four days.

"What about Winthrop?" he continues.

"Hey, don't listen to me."

"Just picking your brain."

"I heard that the over is good."

"What's it at?"

I check the sheets. "One thirty-seven and a half."

"I don't know."

"Neither do I."

I feel awful when this young man goes to the window right in front of me and wagers a total of $440, following my meaning-less advice on Tennessee, Memphis, and the Winthrop over. I follow him to the window and bet $10 on Tennessee only be-cause Harrah's, unlike the Imperial Palace and Bally's, will not accept a $5 bet.

The word among the amateurs is that there is no great harm in betting large amounts as opposed to smaller sums. One will win the same percentage or lose the same percentage of bets regardless of the size of the wager. If you assume that a wise bet-tor can emerge victorious over a four-day period, betting large sums and winning would be better than wagering smaller sums and winning.

This reasoning does seem wise, but it is sound only if the foun-dational plank is correct, that is, that one can emerge victorious after the weekend. If you leave Las Vegas a loser, then while the percentage of losses will be the same regardless of the average amount bet, the total of the loss will be far greater. If you reason correctly that Las Vegas was built and thrives on losers, not win-ners, someone who bets $440 when I wager $10 is likely to lose forty-four times more than I will.

In the seven years I have been going to Las Vegas for the

tournaments, I've averaged losing, exclusive of hotel costs and air travel expenses, about $50 each year, betting—except in very rare instances—no more than $10 a game. In some years I've come home a winner, and in others I've lost more than $50. If the assumption is correct that no amateur bettor against the spread is likely to be much more successful than another, a person betting $50 a game stands to lose about $250 a year. When you add hotel and travel expenses to this, a trip to March Madness can set one back. This reinforces my belief that the army of bettors who come to Las Vegas this weekend do not see the trip as a business proposition. It's a jaunt, a big party, an excursion, a visit to an amusement park. Most bettors know they are likely to lose and treat their gambling losses simply as the price of the ride.

•••

As I leave Harrah's I meet a gray-haired fellow wearing an Ohio State T-shirt over his large frame. I congratulate him on yesterday's victory but offer my condolences about his team not covering the spread. Just like the Grateful Red bettor I met earlier this morning, this Buckeye tells me that he never bets the spread on Ohio State.

"I might bet the money line now and again. And did have something riding on the money line yesterday, but I never bet the spread with the Buckeyes."

I think I know why, but ask him anyway.

"I am Ohio State. Head to toe. Graduated in seventy-one. My father went to Ohio State. Two cousins went to Ohio State. It's a cliché, I know, but I bleed scarlet. I started following them when Jerry Lucas and John Havlicek played for us. You ever hear of them?"

"Sure," I say. "They played in the pros. Havlicek was great."

"In college Lucas was too. Not bad in the pros either. Jerry started as a sophomore at Ohio State back when sophomores didn't. Now he is into this memory nonsense. But anyway, that's another story.

"Maybe I am seven when I start rooting for the Buckeyes. As far as I am concerned, if we win by one or a hundred and one I am happy. One or a hundred and one—makes no difference to me. I don't bet the spread because I do not want to be rooting so that I am only a winner if we win by a certain amount. It takes the fun out of it. And besides I get nervous for the wrong reasons."

"I know."

"Yesterday was a perfect example. If I bet on the spread, I'm disappointed. Believe me, at the end of that game yesterday I was anything but disappointed. I don't want to be disappointed when the Buckeyes win."

"You bet on other games, don't you?"

"Course. This is Vegas."

"Well, you've got to admit you caught a break yesterday."

"What do you mean?"

"The intentional foul."

The Buckeye shakes his head somberly and soberly. "That was not an intentional foul."

"You're kidding."

"I am not kidding. That was not an intentional foul."

I pause. I marvel at this rationalization. If there ever was an intentional foul, what Greg Oden did yesterday was it. He deliberately and forcefully barreled into the opponent in order to stop the clock. I would think that even a Buckeye fan would have to acknowledge the offense, particularly now that Ohio State had emerged as a victor.

"You really believe that wasn't an intentional foul?" I ask him.

"That was not an intentional foul. And, besides, if you look closely at the replay you'll see that Oden got clocked in that war for the ball after the shot."

"Maybe so. You might have a point there, but you have to admit he nailed that guy to stop the clock."

"That was not an intentional foul. He was going for the ball."

I don't want to, because this guy is serious, but I laugh at this. "He was going for the ball?"

His response to my comment and laughter is friendly. "Look, believe what you want," he chuckles. "That was not an intentional foul."

I'm not going to budge this guy. Besides I don't want to. As far as I am concerned he is the real deal and attractive in this way. He may be an avocational bettor, but he, like many of the people I have met this weekend, is a fan at the core.

I return to the Imperial Palace and ride the escalator up to the sports book. A fellow sprints by, apparently eager to make a wager. His T-shirt reads, "If a tree falls in the forest" on the front and "Do the other trees laugh at it?" on the back. He stumbles but does not fall as he jumps off the escalator and runs toward the betting window. The first game does not start for a half an hour.

At the top of the escalator only twelve people wait in line to get a seat in the ballroom, which has nearly unlimited seating. On Thursday at this time there must have been 150 people on this line. The sports book has more action than at 6:30, but it is nothing like it has been the past three days. Many of the bettors are rolling luggage through the book, making their last bets and preparing to watch final games before flying home.

Leaning against his suitcase and scanning the sheets one guy calls out to me, "You like the Salukis?"

"I don't. They couldn't throw the ball in the ocean on Friday, but what do I know?"

"I like the Salukis. Do you like Memphis?"

"I heard Memphis is a lock."

"I don't like Memphis. You like Winthrop?"

"Really, don't go by me. I've been losing all weekend. But yeah, I like Winthrop."

"I don't like Winthrop," he says. He shakes his head and makes a face. "Don't like Winthrop."

•••

The bartenders are set up in the back of the ballroom, just as they have been all weekend, but they have fewer customers at 9 this morning than on previous days. I truly would have trouble counting how many beers I have consumed this weekend and do not want to add another number to my total, so I find a place at a nearly empty table to watch the Tennessee game.

A fellow sitting near me has the same bet I have, Tennessee laying 2½ over Virginia. We watch the entire game together, and he spends much of it grousing about his rotten luck. With 10 seconds to go and the score 75–74 a Tennessee player needs to make two foul shots for both of us to win by half a point. My companion has a polysyllabic one-word reaction to the second foul shot going in, rendering us a winner: "Hallefuckinglujeh." He says it without any emotion whatsoever.

Mickey

I love my picks for this afternoon. I have Wisconsin minus 6 with the psychic force of a legion of Grateful Red bettors behind me. I have Memphis, who according to my acquaintance at the Aladdin is the lock of all time. I have the Winthrop over, which the other genius at the Aladdin felt I should take and run. In a few minutes I intend to bet on Virginia Tech against a Southern Illinois team that on Friday night could not drop a bar of soap into a bathtub. And in a game that will be played later in the day I have Ron from Bally's choice to win it all, Florida minus 9½ against Purdue, a team from the Big Ten that Don assured me was a conference that sucked. Wisconsin is also from the Big Ten, but I like the Grateful Red shirts.

I scan the scoreboard at Bally's to see if there have been any changes to the line before I place my bet on Virginia Tech. Nearby, a short man is shaking his head and scowling in a way that seems to convey something between victimization and self-hate as he mutters to himself.

"I do not believe this. I do not believe you did this, Mickey. I do not believe this. I do not believe you did this, Mickey."

I ask Mickey what he cannot believe.

"You wanna know?"

"If you want to tell me."

"You really wanna know?"

"Sure."

"You wanna know?"

"I want to know."

"What happened? Okay." He pauses, takes a deep breath, and shakes his head.

"What happened?" I ask again.

And then there is no stopping him. I hear his saga in several iterations for the next fifteen minutes.

"Here's what happens. Right? I'm in Caesars and I scored with Tennessee, so I'm going up to the window to collect. Right? And I pick up a betting sheet while I'm on line. You know where they keep the sheets there?"

"I do."

"Okay. So I pick up the sheet while I'm waiting to collect and I scan the sheet and notice something that stuns me. I should have known, but not me."

"What did you see?"

"I see that the odds on the Purdue–Florida game have changed. Dra-mat-ically. What I'd seen earlier as a nine-and-a-half-point Florida spread has dropped to Florida only laying five."

"Five? I laid nine and a half."

"I know. Listen. I figure I'm not an expert, but I know there is no way Florida does not beat Purdue by less than five. Right? No way. Purdue cannot run with them, cannot shoot, cannot rebound. This is a mismatch of epic proportions. Right?"

I don't think he really wants me to respond so I say nothing.

"Right? Right or wrong?"

"Right."

"Of course right. Epic proportions. Purdue cannot get within five of Florida. It's a goddamn lock. I consider the possibility that someone from Florida might be hurt, but the Gators are so stacked that even if Noah was out they would still cover, right?"

I pause before I realize that that was my cue.

"Right."

"Of course right. Five points against Purdue? Please. I figure something is up, but before it stops being up I want to slap down a hundred bucks on this game, and I figure it is like stealing. I go to the window, collect my winnings from Tennessee, and add that to the hundred.

"Now I have plunked down a hundred and fifty bucks on Florida to cover five points against a Purdue team that does not even belong in the tournament. Does not even belong in the tournament." He pauses. "Purdue beat Arizona Friday, but Arizona sucks. So I slap down a hundred and fifty bucks on the game. I feel very proud of myself and I come here."

"Yeah, so?"

"Yeah so, I get here, check the board, and see that in the ten short minutes it took me to walk across Las Vegas fucking Boulevard, the line on the Purdue–Florida game has again rocketed up to nine and a half."

"Wow. That's a jump. Nine and a half? That's what I have."

"I know, that's what you have. Wait. Listen."

"Okay."

"Okay. So it is up to nine and a half. I think I bet it at five. So I feel like a guy who just made a wad on Wall Street buying a stock at noon at thirteen and a half and finding out before he finishes lunch that because of some thing or the other the stock is now at twenty. I am a wizard, right, having found just the correct interval in which to place my bet. I figure that I bet after people got greedy, plunking down a fortune on Florida driving the spread down, and before 'intelligent' people like me quickly countered that trend, driving the line back up to nine and a half points. Right?"

"Right."

"Of course right." He pauses. "But wrong. Do you know what a shlamazal is?"

"Yes, I do know what a shlamazal is."

"A shlamazal is someone with no luck. Shlamazal. Right here." Mickey pauses and points to himself. "Here's what. I'm standing here, a couple of minutes before you come by, feeling like a smart guy. I take out my betting slip to savor my wisdom and am brought down to earth instantly as I see that I am laying nine and a half, not five."

"Yeah, nine and a half. That's what I have."

"God damn it. I know nine and a half is what you have. Nine and a half is what everybody has. But I saw five on the betting sheet at Caesars and I did not look at my ticket when I got it.

So I am bullshit at what I think is the bait and switch at Caesars. My anger fueled no doubt by the case or two of beer I must have guzzled since Thursday."

"Lotta beer here."

"Lotta beer here."

"So, can you go back to Caesars?"

"Listen, will you? Have you been listening? I'm trying to tell a story here and this guy is not listening." He exhales in exasperation.

"I'm listening."

"Right. Yeah. Well. I'm standing here furious because of what I think is some trick. I yank the line sheet out of my pocket just to prove that I'm right. And then I see what a shlamazal I am."

"What do you mean?"

He leans into me with beady eyes and whispers, uttering each word slowly and distinctly.

"When I thought I was betting on a five-point spread, I was looking at the halftime spreads."

"Oh."

"Oh is right. I bet the game based on the halftime spreads thinking it was the game spreads. Five points was the halftime spread."

"Wow. Sorry."

"A shlamazal. I do not believe it. I do not believe you did this, Mickey."

I really don't know what to say. On the Sunday sheets it is pretty clear that the halftime spreads are not the game spreads. This does not seem like a matter of bad luck.

Except for his mantra, which is losing some of its intensity, no words are exchanged between us for a while. Finally, he asks, "Do you think Florida can cover the nine and a half points?"

I shrug my shoulders.

●●●

We sit down. Mickey tells me the story again, with some variations. I am tired of listening to it so he leans over to someone on the other side of him and begins to relay the tale. The new neighbor appears to be singularly uninterested and stares back at him with a look that screams, "Don't tell me your troubles. I have my own."

Mickey is giving me a headache. I can't take his song of woe another time and he appears ready to sing it again. I tell him I have to hit the head, and while he is a good subject for the book, I take another seat when I return from the lavatory.

Not Worth a Flip

My new neighbor is one of the small percentage of people whom I have been unable to engage in conversation this weekend. His responses are monosyllabic, and I suspect his disdainful grunts are intended to discourage contact. I plan to change seats but before doing so realize that I have not yet placed my wager on the Southern Illinois game. By this time I know that to not have a bet on a game is to be without the credential to be parked in a sports book. Besides, I am still miffed at Southern Illinois' inept display when I had the over with them on Friday night. I want to make sure I get in the bet against them. I walk down the ramp to the betting line at the base of the book. The line is not nearly as long as it had been on Thursday, Friday, or Saturday.

Two women who are clearly senior citizens are ahead of me. They are moaning about their losses. They tell me that they can't pick the games worth a "flip." They are from Savannah, Georgia, and are dressed as if they are going to a matinee. They look out of place among the backward-capped, grungy-denimed, risqué-

T-shirted horde. Nevertheless, they are talking basketball on the queue.

In addition to telling me that they can't select winners worth a flip, they also opine that Maryland, who lost to Butler, and Louisville, who couldn't manage to beat Texas A&M, are also not worth a flip. They have lost a good deal of money because these teams have not played worth a flip.

"We are going with Virginia Tech today," one tells me, "and then that is it for Dixie."

"It's a pick 'em," says her friend.

"A pick 'em," I repeat.

"Ah uhm," they say in unison.

"I am going with Tech as well," I say and repeat my grievance about Southern Illinois not being able to throw the ball in the ocean.

"No team we bet on, let me tell you, can throw the ball in the ocean," one says.

"You lose a lot of money?"

Their interesting response supports what seems to be the attitude of many of the bettors. "Yes," they shrug, "but on Monday we'll go back to work and make more." I could be wrong, but these people are spending play money on this trip.

•••

I walk up the ramp, through the bar, and out of Bally's sports book. I intend to go through the casino and through the Paris in order to get to the Aladdin, where I have decided to watch the games. I never get there. On the way I spot a gathering of Wisconsin fans and decide to join this crew.

The Grateful Red are assembled in a lounge near where Bally's and the Paris are joined. This viewing area probably has no more than a hundred seats. The lounge is not intended to be a sports book, but like the comedy stage at Harrah's it has been appropriated this weekend to accommodate March Madness overflow. Four large television monitors have been placed in the lounge, and nearly all one hundred of the comfortable lounge chairs are filled not primarily with bettors but with Wisconsin fans adorned in team gear primed to cheer for the Grateful Red. Even though I'm out of costume, I join the Badgers. Since no seat is available, I lean against a metal barrier around the lounge.

At the moment the lounge is as depressing as a funeral home, with the Grateful Red quietly staring at the four screens. The Badgers are done. Not only will they not cover the 6-point spread, the University of Nevada at Las Vegas will defeat them outright on the money line. I wonder if Roger had UNLV on one of his dog money line parlays. Nobody in this group did. Members of the Grateful Red are whispering to each other sadly, as if they've lost a relative.

Having lost my first bet of the afternoon, I think of the maniac who kept muttering "Friggin' Cheeseheads" by the poker machine. One of the Grateful Red seated on the other side of the rail is shaking his head. He looks to be fifty years old.

"Tough game," I say.

"This spot is not working out for me."

"What do you mean?"

"Sat here for Virginia, Tennessee. Guy hits both foul shots. Lost that. Now this. Seat is not lucky."

"Must be the seat."

"Stranger things to believe in," he says.

"You superstitious?"

"Some. Wear the same socks to every home game."

"Do you wash them?"

"Of course, I wash them. What, do you think I'm crazy?" He

knows this is funny before he says it. He is laughing at himself. "Maybe I am crazy."

"Nah."

"Maybe."

I decide not to proceed to the Aladdin. I do not want to miss too much of the other games on which I have wagered. Also, I don't want to stand next to such an unlucky seat while I still have three good bets that are still alive: Virginia Tech against the Salukis brick-layers, the "take it and run" Winthrop over, and "the lock of all time" with Memphis.

The Wilsons

In Bally's I find a seat in a prime location. On the counter above the seat is a sign that reads "Reserved for Wilson." The counters above the three adjacent seats in this row also read "Reserved for Wilson." No Wilsons are around so I take a vacant chair. Shortly thereafter a forty-year-old man arrives armed with a large plastic container that smells like breakfast. Right behind him is his dead ringer, only twenty-five years older. The older man also carries a large plastic container. The two are dressed for casual Friday in a business firm. The younger man wears a powder blue cotton golf shirt and navy blue pressed slacks. The older one—who must be the young man's father—wears a similar top in white and the kind of green slacks you would see in a retail store specializing in golfing equipment.

These must be Wilsons, I figure. They sit down at two of the empty chairs and glance at me as if I am the same sort of riffraff they have been shooing away for four days. I see no more Wil-sons on the horizon and remain seated.

Wilson junior looks like he has not budged from his spot except to get provisions for four days. He is very serious. He places his breakfast carton to his right and opens up a folder akin to the loose-leaf notebooks I have seen throughout this weekend.

His is remarkably neat. Clipped to his folder are four pens: a blue highlighter, a yellow highlighter, and two fancy ball point pens. He does not carry a cheap Bic pen. His loose-leaf is thick, not as thick as a dictionary, but it looks to contain about three hundred pages of basketball data. Like others I have seen, his book is divided neatly into sections. On a separate clipboard he has attached the tournament bracket sheet. I can see that he has, very neatly, recorded the victors on the bracket sheet, inking in the results.

Wilson junior does not appear to be interested in talking with me much, but I am able to discover, with some persistent questioning, that when he records the victors on the bracket sheet he highlights his winning bets in blue and the losers in yellow. From my vantage point, there seems to be much more yellow than blue on the page. The Wilsons exchange very few words, occasionally smirking when something outlandish occurs that undermines their betting interests. The smirks seem to be their shorthand for "Can you believe how we are getting shafted by this conspiracy of fools?"

The Wilsons consume their meals carefully. I wonder if they have ever put too much ketchup on a hamburger, causing some to drip on their fingers when they take a bite. I figure I could make a bundle in Vegas betting against that. I cannot tell for sure if Wilson junior is basically quiet or snooty. I give him the benefit of the doubt and tell him about my project. I ask him a question or two, but his responses are terse, condescendingly so. I wonder if they are losing a bundle or if they have just had it dealing with philistines. The periodic shouts of "You suck!" and "He walked!" and "You gotta be fucking kidding me!" are obnoxious even to me, particularly when they seem to be fueled by excessive alcohol consumption, but these two react to some of the more profane outbursts as if someone has squirted a water

gun in their face and they would love to be able to hail security
to clean the place out.

Judging by their reactions, mostly nonverbal, the Wilsons
have Winthrop plus 3½ in their game with Oregon. This is not
good news for the Wilsons. Winthrop is being throttled, the 3½
points do not look like they will be nearly enough, and Wilson
junior will soon have to reach for the yellow highlighter.

Sometime during the second half a woman about Wilson junior's age and another woman about Wilson senior's age stop by.
They have been shopping, they say. The younger one asks "How
are you boys doing?" Wilson junior manages a weak smile. Wilson senior's smile is a little broader. The conversation between
Wilson junior and the younger woman—his wife—is taking
place very close to where I sit. It includes a good deal of "honey"
this and "honey" that—exchanged perfunctorily, it seems. Both
men attempt to be attentive to their spouses while stealing looks
at the television screens that inform them of whether they will
be able to pull their weight when it comes time to pay the mortgage. It looks doubtful. After a spell the elder woman departs,
wishing her "boys" good luck. The younger woman lingers a
while longer before giving her man a kiss that would be sanc-
tioned by ultraconservatives in the religious right. When she
eventually leaves I wonder if this couple has any better chance
of marital happiness than the drunk newlyweds I met earlier this
morning.

The Wilsons have no hope of winning their spread bet on
Winthrop, but like me, they also have a wager on the over in the
game. This over is the one that the Aladdin fellow had told me
to "take and run." A lock. The Wilsons and I are still alive with
the over, but it has turned out to be nothing akin to a lock.

I do not know how many consecutive games the Wilsons have
lost but if their facial expressions are an indication, the women

from Savannah are doing better. The Wilsons are very tight at the last moments of the Winthrop game. The over is 137½, and with seconds remaining the score is 75–61, 136 points. Winthrop has the ball with plenty of time to take a shot and bring the total to 138. Oregon is not playing any defense. As far as Oregon is concerned the game is over. Winthrop can't overcome 14 points in 15 seconds, so the Oregon players are content to stand on the court like mannequins and allow Winthrop to score while the seconds expire. Consequently, any player for Winthrop could drive to the basket, make an uncontested shot, and render the Wilsons and me winners.

I am certain that the Wilsons have more money on the line than I do, so I can understand their muffled moan when Winthrop passes on an open layup and hoists up a low-percentage 3-point shot. It misses. Winthrop obtains the rebound. Again, they can shoot an uncontested layup. They do not. The Winthrop rebounder passes the ball back out beyond the 3-point line.

For the first time Wilson junior shows some emotion. He slams his hand on the table, still careful to avoid the remnants of breakfast and his notebooks.

"Dunk the ball," he fumes.

A Winthrop player attempts another 3-point shot. Again it clanks off the rim. The Wilsons smirk, shake their heads, and look at each other. "Can you believe how we are getting shafted by this conspiracy of idiots?"

But it is not over for me and the Wilsons. Oregon players are not contesting even the rebounds. Winthrop secures the ball after the missed shot. A five-year-old could make a shot given the resistance from Oregon. A made shot would bring the total to 138 and would allow Wilson junior to reach for the blue. But the Winthrop player who grabbed the rebound does not take the

shot a five-year-old could make. Instead he dribbles the ball behind the 3-point arc. Wilson senior stands up. "No!" he shouts.
"No!"

Winthrop chucks up a third consecutive 3-point shot. And
they miss it as time expires. The total points remain at 136, 1½
points short of what is necessary for our "take it and run" over.
Wilson junior turns his head to the side as if he has just taken a
slap to the face. It might appear to people seated behind us that
he is looking at me, but he is not. His face is rigid as he stares
into the distance at some land of peace where he can use a blue
highlighter. He turns back around to face forward and rubs a
single finger on his well-shaved chin.

Wilson senior eventually sits down. He slides his hands back
and forth on top of his green-slacked thighs. He removes one
hand and with it takes his thumb and forefinger and pulls down
on his nose several times. He gazes angrily ahead, as if he has
been wronged once again by some evil force.

I lose the bet also, but I am not hurting like the Wilsons. They
do not converse much and have not moved discernibly by the time
the older Wilson woman jauntily returns to the row. She has a
grandmotherly smile and asks a variation of the question earlier
posed by her daughter-in-law: "How are my boys doing?"

I cannot hear a response.

● ● ●

The Southern Illinois game is concluding. Southern Illinois can,
all of a sudden, throw the ball in the ocean. They score 63 points
and hold Virginia Tech to only 48. Apparently I, the Wilsons,
and the women from Savannah cannot pick teams worth a flip.
I lose my third of the three games completed thus far this afternoon—all of which I thought were can't miss bets.

The only thing I salvage is the Memphis game. They win easily against Nevada, just as the expert in the Aladdin had predicted.

Wilson junior budges. He has taken out his blue highlighter and almost appears smug.

"You have Memphis?" I ask.

"Of course," he says still not smiling. "Memphis was a lock."

• • •

The man I first spotted on Wednesday when I chatted with Arnie from Dallas by way of Trenton is sitting at the far edge of the sports book. On Wednesday he had been rambling to himself when he was not nodding out. He is in the same spot and conscious at the moment, and he is still talking to himself. I walk over to him. He is providing a running play-by-play of the action, as if he is a broadcaster doing a recap of the afternoon's activity.

"So Memphis prevails, covers easily, needing five and a half and clobbering Nevada by sixteen. I am a winner with Memphis. Winthrop bet is a loser however . . ."

By the Hook

I am becoming tired of all of this. I am about to watch my forty-sixth, forty-seventh, and forty-eighth basketball game in four days, not including the professional contest I watched on Friday night in an attempt to salvage at least something from that evening. I wonder if, in general, the fatigue that I am feeling is shared by others and has manifested itself in unattractive behavior. The Wilsons may well have been snobbish and distant whenever I might have made their acquaintance, and the fellow talking to himself had been in a world of his own since he first pitched his tent on Wednesday night—assuming he is not that way regularly during the year regardless of the context.

Yet the combination of watching the many games, the reduction in the numbers of people cheering, and the residual effects of the beer seems to have had a deflating effect on everyone in Bally's sports book. The other man I saw on Wednesday when I first arrived at Bally's is sitting in the exact same spot he had as before. He had smiled at me then, and does so again, but this time it is forced. My guess is that his look is not strained because of a series of defeats but more due to the wear and tear of continuous viewing.

• • •

I find a new seat at the top of the amphitheater, several rows back from the Wilsons, very close to where I had been chatting with Ron just last night.

A very serious no-fun guy who is unwilling to engage in conversation sits to my right. He is watching the Florida–Purdue contest with something far more than casual interest. He is so intense that I wonder if he might be a professional bettor, but I sense it is more likely that he's betting more than he should or that he has lost more than he should and badly needs this game.

I know he is pulling for Purdue, because when Purdue scores a 3-point basket he clenches his fist and mutters something that sounds like Marv Albert saying "Yes!" I cannot tell precisely what he is saying because his mouth is shut so tightly that no sound is clearly discernible. I wonder if he has the rent or more riding on his bet. Toward the end of the game, Purdue scores a basket, but the television graphic indicates that the goal was scored by Florida. Any casual observer of sports on television knows that this error occurs now and then and that it is always corrected. Nevertheless the mistake incenses my neighbor. He stands up and chastises cbs profanely, excoriating the television set three thousand miles from where the game was being played.

"That was Purdue, you goddamn asshole!"

He takes his seat slowly, obviously steamed.

"Can't keep the fucking score straight," he spews to no one in particular as he keeps his eyes riveted on the screen.

As Mickey discovered earlier today, the spread on this game is not the halftime spread of 5 points, but 9½. The tense man is in good shape as Purdue has been hanging around and making it close throughout. Nevertheless, he reacts to every Florida score as if each is a dagger that has been thrust into his ribs. He closes his eyes and grimaces with each bucket, periodically muttering, "They're gonna blow it. I know they're gonna blow it."

The final is 74–67. I lose my bet as does Mickey, but my neighbor wins and because of that even I feel like I can exhale. I congratulate him. For the first time in an hour he says something civil to me. His face does not break out in a smile, but it does betray evidence of relief.

"They make you sweat for every dollar," he says, exhausted.

I vow that if I ever get close to being like this guy I will know that the fun has stopped. Even in victory he does not seem to be having a good time.

•••

Poor Mickey. With a spread of 5 points he would have been a winner, but the 9½ spread and the 74–67 outcome has set him back $150. I shake my head as I remember his song of woe and his oft-repeated refrain. I am still thinking about his mutterings when I am poked from the back. It is Mickey. He has not missed a beat.

"Do you believe that?" he asks. "Do you believe how Mickey messed up?"

I want to evaporate but have nowhere to go. I consider taking another stab at saying I have to go to the men's room, but I fear that what he will do is tell me about some intestinal virus that once kept him bedridden for months. He sits next to me. I have to hear the story again. He tells me that he has the under in the Kansas–Kentucky game. This is another sad sack bet. Kentucky and Kansas are scoring easily and the under has almost no chance to be a winner.

Mickey does arithmetic in an attempt to assess his slim chances for victory: If both teams have scored X points in Y minutes, how many points will they score in 40 minutes? I wonder if my enjoyment for March Madness would dwindle, if not dissipate, if the only wagers I made were over-unders, because then the contest itself is completely lost. There is no competition. When you bet the under or over you are hoping for cooperation in a game that is founded on contention.

At some point Mickey realizes that it is no use. These teams cannot possibly score less than 140. He gets the betting slip from his wallet and freezes.

"Look at this, Al. Look at this."

Mickey has inadvertently wagered on the over, not the under. This error has made him a winner. He is stunned, almost unwilling to accept his good fortune.

"Mickey thought he bet the under," he says.

"You bet the over."

"Mickey wanted to bet the under."

"This is great. You win."

"Finally. Mickey the shlamazal catches a break." He is quick to point out that he lost more on the earlier gaffe than he gained by this error, but he is relieved nonetheless.

I am amused more by the irony in this than by anything else. All weekend I've thought more and more frequently that handicapping these games is unlikely to be helpful, and one might do just as well by guessing. Mickey made two bets on this last group of games that were based on faulty logic. In one case he thought the halftime spread was the game spread, and in the other he accidentally bet on the under when he wanted to bet on the over. I believe that the vast number of amateurs who are attending these games would do no better or poorly if they selected their bets by tossing a coin or consulting their grandmothers.

Mickey stumbles out of his chair. "That is it for Mickey. Time to quit with that luck."

We shake hands. I congratulate him again on his blind good fortune. He smiles and pauses.

"Next year, it's going to be different," he says.

•••

A fellow sits where the pensive Purdue bettor had been. He is far more gregarious than his predecessor. We talk about how many times the outcome seems to be close to the spread number. It seems truly astounding how frequently the spreads were on target: the outcome of twenty-two percent of the forty-eight games would have changed if a 3-point basket had been made at the end of the game.

My new neighbor, who is in town not to watch basketball but because he is the commissioner of a fantasy baseball league, informs me that several games this weekend were decided by the hook.

"By the hook?" I say. "What is the hook?"

The hook, I discover, is gambling slang that refers to the half point in the spread. For example, those who bet on Ohio State giving 7½ lost by the hook when the final was 78–71. I had not heard this expression used before. My baseball commissioner friend begins to discuss college basketball.

"You watch a lot of college basketball in a short period of time and the types of offenses become very similar. Either you are trying to score a short layup from one of the angles around the hoop, or you are trying to set up a three. Very few shots are taken from anywhere else. A short jump shot is a low-percentage shot compared to a longer one. When you see someone take a midrange jumper, after watching forty-plus games, it looks clearly like an anomaly."

This analysis is interrupted by someone below us who, apparently not out of gas from the weekend, stands up and screams, "Texas! You suck!"

This exclamation notwithstanding, Texas must not suck too badly. They easily defeat Southern California in the forty-eighth game of this forty-eight-game weekend.

● ● ●

When the Texas game ends, winning bettors get up slowly to form the last line of the weekend and collect on their wagers. Stragglers remain at littered tables reviewing their slips. Others pack up their notebooks. The Wilsons pack their materials in a suitcase like businessmen leaving the office for the day.

Two friends walk behind where I am seated.

"I am pulling for Florida all the way," says one.

"Ah. But they didn't fucking cover," laments his buddy.

Other people who have been parked at Bally's all weekend begin shaking hands goodbye. The aisles are crammed with suitcases.

The screens at Bally's are not dark: a women's basketball game is on, with Sean McDonough doing the play-by-play.

Over the last four days I have been in the Imperial Palace, Bally's, Treasure Island, the Venetian, the Mirage, Caesars,

Bellagio, Paris, MGM, Bill's, O'Shea's, the Flamingo, Aladdin, Harrah's, and the Monte Carlo.

I am whipped.

Leaving Bally's sports book on my way to the Imperial Palace where my luggage is stored, I go through the casino floor one more time. The same Hollywood cardboard character extras crowd the blackjack tables, roulette wheels, and one-armed bandits who were there on Wednesday. The same squeals of victory and the same casino music can be heard. Everything is the same. Nothing has changed.

On the Strip only a few bettors stare at line sheets, but tourists still stagger by holding plastic cups filled with booze. Another of the twenty-four-hour happy hours at O'Shea's is in full swing. At the Imperial Palace I wave goodbye to Buddy Holly as if we are good friends. He waves back to me as well.

The Aussies

It is Sunday early evening. I am gassed. I relax in a hot tub with a fellow who is both a tour guide and van driver for tourists. The driver tells me about his life and how his job has taken him all over and how he has seen "pretty much everything." He tells me I can buy a house on the sea in a town called Constantine in Romania for a song and about other beyond-my-world adventures. We are joined in the hot tub by a woman who lives in Portugal and then three Australians on the trip. The Aussies are wild. They are looking to get drunk and find prostitutes. The woman from Portugal is older than these Aussies and finds their sophomoric interests more amusing than offensive.

"Are you sure you fellows will know what to do when you find your dates?"

This sets the Aussies laughing hysterically. They make a series of bawdy comments about what they will do. They continue to ask the van driver many questions about boozing, strip joints, and the protocol for approaching dancers for sex. This wild talk seems bizarre to me, like overhearing people plotting a crime. The Aussies continue to talk about how drunk they will get and how they will solicit sex.

Eventually the Aussies calm down, the woman from Portugal stops teasing and giggling at them, and the van driver ceases to expound on the value of Constantine real estate.

They ask me what I am doing in Las Vegas.

When I tell them that I just spent five days sitting in casinos watching forty-eight basketball games they are politely incredulous.

"Why would anyone want to do that?" asks one of the Aussies without emotion. Gone is the almost hysterical tone that characterized the narrative describing his lascivious evening plans.

I try to explain the March Madness scene. I describe some of the characters I met. I explain how the spread makes every game an exciting toss-up.

The five others in the hot tub who have either just described or listened to wacky, dangerous, possibly illegal behavior stare at me baffled.

I finish my description.

"Cool," says the van driver evenly, but he does not mean it.

•••

I have a red-eye flight back to Boston. I leave the hot tub, dress, gather my belongings, and get on the cab line with the Hollywood extras who have been standing there all weekend to provide a backdrop for this show. In a few minutes two fellows get behind me whom I've seen at the Imperial Palace during the weekend. I had not talked to them previously, but they, like I, had watched the games. I figure I can save a few dollars on the cab ride and ask them if they want to share a cab to the airport. They agree.

These two have not fared well betting on the games.

"I don't want to count up how much I lost," says one. "I lost Ohio State. I lost Pittsburgh. I lost Winthrop. I lost Virginia."

"We both lost, Jamie."

"Unbelievable. Couldn't pick a winner."

I commiserate. The silence is broken by Jamie.

"Next year it's going to be different," he says.

•••

I have plenty of time at the JetBlue terminal before my flight back to Boston. I arrived early to avoid congestion that might cause me to miss my plane. I don't want to return to the Strip for another day. There is a limit to how much one can enjoy of this fantasyland, and I have reached it.

Wireless Internet is free at McCarran International Airport, so I find a place to plug in my laptop and catch up on e-mail, then start typing up some of my notes on the weekend. Three men congregating behind me look like they've spent the last four days in sports books. They wear tired-looking T-shirts and need a shave. Two of them have on cargo shorts, no doubt employed this weekend to separate winning from hopeful betting slips and to hold line sheets. The third wears a pair of jeans that appear to have survived a forty-mile hike.

They don't notice me at first as they huddle in a row behind me. One yanks out a stenographer's notebook from a pocket on his shorts. The one with the ratty jeans pulls a loose-leaf notebook from his knapsack. A fortnight is left in the tournament: next week the sixteen teams who have survived this weekend—referred to as the Sweet Sixteen—will compete to be among the Final Four, who will play during the last weekend of March Madness. The boys behind me are handicapping next week's games.

"How did you do?" I ask.

Two of the three wave a "Don't ask."

"Not bad," the third says. "I hit a parlay on Saturday that these chumps didn't have the rocks to bet."

"Yeah, go figure that Pitt was going to choke like the Chargers," said one of his friends.

"I figured," said the winner.

"You from San Diego?" I ask.

"Go to school there."

"I see you're checking out the Sweet Sixteen."

"Yeah. We're coming back next week. Driving. Next week we're going to win big." The three laugh at themselves.

"Seriously," the guy in jeans continues, "this week we got to see what was going on. See the lay of the land. Next week. We feel pretty good about next week."

One of the friends sees that I have been at work on my laptop.

"Whatcha doing?"

I tell them.

"Whoa. Good idea. Some crazy stuff out there."

They go back to handicapping their games and I go back to typing. One of them pokes me.

"Yo doc."

"Yes."

"You like Florida to cover the seven against Butler?"

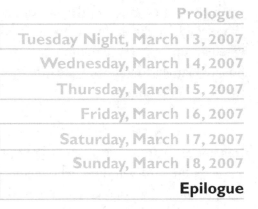

Prologue

Tuesday Night, March 13, 2007

Wednesday, March 14, 2007

Thursday, March 15, 2007

Friday, March 16, 2007

Saturday, March 17, 2007

Sunday, March 18, 2007

Epilogue

2 to 1 in 508

Larry Poppel, my dear childhood friend, is a very serious hockey fan. His team is the New York Rangers, and he follows them so much that he worries about them.

I do not share my friend's enthusiasm. Of the major team sports, hockey is actually my least favorite. But to support him I occasionally travel down to New York to sit with him in his season tickets in section 508 in Madison Square Garden.

Section 508 (I have changed the section number and the occupants' names) is populated by knowledgeable, loyal, enthusiastic fans, just like Larry. They go to the games, not like people out for an evening's entertainment, but rather like blue-collar employees showing up for work. Instead of lunch pails they lug their affection for the Rangers as they assemble, slide into their seats, collectively take a deep breath, hoist up their jeans, and prepare to watch their beloved team.

Before 1994 the New York Rangers and their fans had endured the humiliation of not winning a championship in fifty-four years. Fans of opponents would often insult the Rangers by regularly jeering "1940, 1940" when opportunities presented themselves. Nevertheless, despite the taunts and past failures, every single night during a hockey season the steadfastly devoted group in 508 would lumber up to the top tier of Madison Square Garden to join with the others in the arena to cheer for the New York Rangers.

• • •

It is not uncommon for people to refer to fervid sports fanatics as "get a lifers." Even those who enjoy sports comment disparagingly about fans who cannot seem to get out of bed without worrying about the health of a goalie or whether a high school basketball star will be successfully recruited to play for a favorite university. Saying "get a life" to people fretting about such issues has become a way to suggest that there are other matters to consider in the world and that enthusiasm for sports can lead to a loss of perspective.

For example, I once heard a listener call in to a talk radio show and rant about an outfielder who had a tendency to play without enthusiasm. This laziness, according to the caller, turned singles into doubles and allowed runners on first to get to third easily. The caller was hoarse from shouting. In the course of his tirade, there was an audible crash and rumble in the background.

The broadcaster interrupted the caller and asked, "What was that?"

"Ah, my wife tripped over a wire and fell down some stairs," the caller responded evenly, then without pausing continued rasping, "It really burns my butt when Strawberry won't hustle after the single."

Aghast, the talk show host shouted "Sir, take care of your wife and get a life!"

For far less egregious behaviors the likes of the rabid folks in 508 have also heard the admonition to "get a life."

•••

In 1994 the Rangers seemed to have a legitimate chance to take home the coveted Stanley Cup, the symbol of the National Hockey League championship. In each prior year when Larry would talk optimistically about chances for the Cup even he knew there was really no possibility of obtaining it. But in 1994 the Rangers had progressed easily through the first two playoff series, sweeping the hated New York Islanders and beating the Washington Capitols four games to one. The Rangers would play the New Jersey Devils in the penultimate round of the play-offs. If the Rangers could defeat the Devils, they would likely play a weaker opponent in the finals. The Devils seemed to present the only legitimate hurdle to winning the Cup. To the season ticket holders in section 508, a Stanley Cup would be, literally, a dream come true.

Unfortunately, as the series with the Devils proceeded, the dream of winning the Stanley Cup seemed as if it would turn out to be yet another agonizing illusion for Ranger fans. After five games, the Devils led the best-of-seven series three games to two and were playing the sixth game on their home ice. After two periods of the sixth game, they led the Rangers by a score of 3–1. My friend Larry was beyond depressed. He shut his television off at the end of the second period and urged his wife Angie to join him and go to sleep. Larry could not take watching a third period that resulted, once again, in a Cup-less Ranger season. He told Angie that if the Rangers were to miraculously overcome the 3–1 deficit and win, I would call and wake them up.

I called. The Rangers had stormed back in the third period to win the sixth game. The ringing phone rousted Larry from his forced slumber. When he heard my voice he reacted with stunned, but joyous, disbelief. He repeated my report in ecstatic short rasps to Angie. "The Rangers won! They came back! They won!"

Then he said, "Al, you gotta come down for the seventh game."

•••

On May 27, 1994, the Friday of Memorial Day weekend, I drove to New York and met Larry and Angie in a bar called Charlie O's, which sits at the entrance to Madison Square Garden. On this night—two hours before the opening face-off of the seventh game—Charlie O's was jammed wall to wall with keyed-up Ranger fans.

Larry told me that he and I would not be sitting next to each other for this game. In order to accommodate me as well as Angie, he had secured two seats from another season ticket holder. He and Angie would use the other tickets and sit in the tonier mezzanine section. I would be in hardscrabble 508 with a hockey pal of his named Richie. "Wait till you meet Richie," Larry said. "He's quite a character." To be "quite a character" among the population in section 508 would be no small achievement. Richie did not disappoint. At six feet tall and no more than 150 pounds, wearing a beat-up felt hat, he reminded me of Ed Norton from *The Honeymooners*. With his lid not quite fitting securely on his head, he wiggled through the crowd at Charlie O's carrying a briefcase. He gave Angie a big hug and kiss, bear-hugged Larry, then looked at me. "You must be Poppel's friend."

"Yes."

"Ranger fan?"

"Tonight I am."

"Better be, Poppel's friend. Better be."

• • •

Larry's season tickets were in the very front row of section 508, the fifth and sixth seats in from the aisle. I took the sixth seat and Richie settled into the fifth. Directly in front of us was a three-foot-tall brick wall with a metal guardrail, then a walkway used by media personnel and photographers. For this deciding seventh game, folding chairs had been set up in the space to allow for additional spectators. Among the people sitting in the folding chairs was a cluster of nuns. I wondered how they might react to the language that I knew would be cascading from our section during the course of this evening.

Seated to my right was a bull of a man. Not especially tall, maybe only five feet eight, but he looked like he lived in a gym. This rock-hard fellow was all business. I tried to get him to converse, but he was too tense and focused. I managed to eke out that he lived in Albany, drove the 120 miles down just for the game, and that he and his family were moving the next day to a new house.

"You're moving tomorrow? Your wife okay with that? I mean is your wife okay about you coming down for the game since you're moving tomorrow?"

"No. She is not okay," he said. He did not seem to want to elaborate on this issue or anything else. He was staring straight ahead at the ice.

Before the game a tall, broad-shouldered photographer walked behind the nuns in the aisle just below where Richie, I, and the guy from Albany were rooted. The photographer had closely cropped hair and a receding hairline, that, combined with the shape of his head, gave him an unusually expansive forehead. He was calm and relaxed, in stark contrast to the agitated people around me.

"You a fan, or just working?" I asked him.

"Just working. Hockey? Don't think so." He shook his head. "I don't know what you all see in this game."

"Just snapping pictures?"

"Just snapping pictures."

"Don't care if the Rangers win?"

"Just snapping pictures."

Right before the game began Richie repeatedly folded and unfolded his arms, stretched out his hands, and tapped the metal railing in front of us.

"What is that?" I asked him, referring to his ritualistic movements.

"Just a little something I do."

I stared at him.

"Works best on metals," he said by way of explanation.

●●●

It was not until the second period that the first goal of this seventh game was scored. To the relieved joy of everyone around me, the Rangers made the score, and it stood up throughout the period. When I went to the men's room during the intermission I stood at the back of a long line of fans, nearly all of whom were adorned in Ranger uniforms. From the queue, an ear-splitting chant of "Let's go Rangers, let's go!" blasted against the tiles. At one point, the cheering lost some of its intensity. "Come on!" screamed one of the faithful. "They need us now. Don't give up. They need us now!" The chant picked right up again.

The tension in Madison Square Garden throughout the third period was truly palpable. It seemed as if every few minutes, Richie did his arm-folding and hand-tapping ritual on the railing. The Albany muscle man stared straight ahead and had not said more than three words to me since our initial exchange before the first period.

The thin 1–0 lead continued to hold up as the minutes and seconds drained off the clock. The fans in section 508 were wide-eyed and nearly delirious. This could be it. The Rangers might win this seventh game, and then go on to play the lesser-talented Vancouver Canucks, a team that could and would be defeated in the finals. The Rangers might win the Stanley Cup. Now there was only 1 minute left. Now 30 seconds. Now 15 seconds. Ten, nine, eight . . .

With 7.7 seconds left and the arena ready to burst with unrestrained glee, the Devils scored a goal, sending the game into overtime.

I have never heard such silence. Richie moaned as if he had been shot. Albany's eyes flared. He looked like someone who had been waiting to see a sign on the New York State Thruway that read "Albany 10 miles," but when he approached the marker saw that it read "Albany 1,000 miles." During the intermission before the overtime period, Ranger fans walked the corridors in a daze. One man used his left hand to prop up his right arm. Blood oozed from his knuckles. Someone asked, "Are you okay? What's wrong?"

"I punched the wall. That's what's wrong. 'Am I okay?' The Devils scored with seven seconds left. Am I okay, this guy wants to know."

In the Stanley Cup playoffs, tied games are resolved by a procedure called sudden death. Additional 20-minute periods are played until a goal is scored, resulting in an immediate victory. If no team scores in the first extra period, the teams take a break, return to the ice, and play a second sudden death period. This process continues until a team scores a deciding goal.

For every zealot in Madison Square Garden on that night, the sudden death period in the arena was beyond tense. Any shot taken by the New Jersey Devils could mark the end of the game, series, and Stanley Cup hopes. Every time the Devils secured the puck and began skating toward the Ranger net, the air was sucked out of the Garden. And every time the Rangers skated back the other way there was hope that maybe the result of this rush would be a victory.

Neither team scored during the first overtime period. I am not a hockey fan, but I was limp with exhaustion. During the intermission, diehards flopped dizzily around the concourses like noodles. After the first few rushes of the second overtime, I began to get pains in my chest. I tried to remind myself that I did not even like hockey, but this did not seem to help. The nuns were fiddling with something in front of me. At one point the Devils raced up the ice and unleashed a screaming slap shot that the Ranger goalie managed heroically to kick away at the last second. The puck went careening into the stands and play was temporarily halted. The whole arena gasped. Joe Cool the photographer wheezed and wheeled around, no longer a dispassionate observer. Beads of sweat sparkled on his broad forehead.

"Wow. That was close. Wow," he said.

Prior to the ensuing face-off I said something to myself that I had muttered throughout my life on occasion, but had never previously meant literally: "I don't know how much more of this I can take." I started thinking about what would happen if the Devils scored a goal. The place would crumble. I tried to imagine how the explosion of energy might manifest itself. There had to be a winner and a loser in this game. If the Rangers were to lose, Larry, Richie, and the nineteen thousand others in the arena would be crushed.

I had to calm myself. I imagined scenes in my life that were particularly comforting. I thought about my nephew's fifth birthday party, when he decided to give a sweet if nonsensical speech to all assembled. I remembered a day at the beach with a sweetheart many years before. We were running pass patterns in the sand, tossing a beanbag like a football back and forth. I tried to remember the sound of the ocean that day and the serenity of the waves . . .

MATTEAU, MATTEAU, MATTEAU, MATTEAU, MATTEAU, MATTEAU!

A Ranger player named Stephane Matteau had scored. Matteau had taken the puck at the side of the net and stuffed it past the Devil goaltender.

The Garden erupted.

Immediately and with no thought to the contrary I turned to Richie and we embraced. An instant later I did what came extraordinarily naturally, I wheeled around to my silent Albany neighbor—a person with whom I had exchanged less than twenty-five words in my life—and proceeded to share as ferocious a hug as any I have ever or will share. We all laughed and teared as we walked up the aisle to exit. Everyone high-fived each other. It felt like the entire Garden was celebrating the birth of a baby. Richie and I met up with Angie and Larry when we got to the ground level and embraced as if we were at their wedding. People cried in the lobby as they hugged their friends.

We decided to stop for a beer. We found a bar that was populated with other Ranger fans clad in their jerseys. We grabbed a table, ordered a pitcher, and observed the scene. Limp Ranger fanatics shook their heads, gazing at replays of the final goal on a television set propped above the bar. As I looked around at the group it seemed that there was enough sweat on their jerseys to convince someone that these guys themselves had skated some shifts. They were elated, wildly happy, drinking, toasting, tearing—this sudden death victory in a seventh game.

•••

This scene in the bar—this frozen image of elated people bliss-fully enjoying the moment—regularly came to mind as I re-searched and wrote this book. To feel those Ranger fans' pas-sion and love and sense of belonging was special, something to be envied and emulated. The people I met in Las Vegas during March Madness also had a passion. Sure, it took them to Las Vegas so they could sit in sports books for sixteen hours on four consecutive days to watch forty-eight basketball games, to race to get on line for a seat two hours before the doors opened, to fill huge loose-leaf notebooks with data and shape it into a system, to throw pencils at television sets after someone missed a free throw, to wear red or green or blue or gold from head to toe, and to come back and do it all over again year after year. Sure, it was crazy, but they had found something that thrilled them, something they loved.

And it often occurred to me that the people who demurely sit through the days and weeks and months, who never become excited about anything, who never find or seek a place to re-charge their emotional energy—it is these people, not the deliri-ous sports fans and crazed March Madness bettors, who would be wise indeed to hurry up and get a life.

Acknowledgments

I could not have completed this book without the support and assistance of many individuals. First, I want to thank Rob Taylor at the University of Nebraska Press, who expressed interest in the project, encouraged me to refine the proposal, and supported the work that resulted in the book that you now hold. Rob's comments on the manuscript and his tactfully communicated recommendations made this book far superior to what it otherwise would have been.

Major thanks to my high school friend, Gary Aaronson, who read both the original prospectus and an initial version of the manuscript. Gary, a successful and busy accountant—and a sports aficionado—took several of his precious hours to read the book and provided valuable feedback and encouragement. Others who read sections and provided their insights include Ken Turow, Dr. Robert Zaremba, Meaghan Sinclair, Leah Hatten, Abby Tremblay, Angela Chin, and Hunter Wells. Helen Goodman, a longtime special friend, read several sections and offered support at many stages of the writing, for which I am more than grateful.

I could not have had the insights to the behind-the-scenes

nature of the sports book operation without the willing assistance of the three managers who agreed to be interviewed for this book. Two of these three requested anonymity and I have protected their anonymity throughout, but you know who you are and I thank you both very much. Mike Fay at the Imperial Palace was very considerate, kind, and helpful, as were members of his staff. The Imperial Palace is an outstanding venue for watching March Madness games. They treat their customers with respect and consideration and try to ensure a positive experience for all those who visit the sports book. No doubt Mike was in large part responsible for creating this environment. In addition to the Imperial Palace, readers will know that during 2007 I spent time in the Venetian, Bally's, Paris, and Caesars Palace. Each experience was positive. Staff members at these hotels were unaware of my work on the book. I was treated no differently than the average customer, and I was treated very well. Also thanks to Dr. David Schwartz, the very successful author of books on the history of gambling and the director of the Center for Gaming Studies at UNLV. Dr. Schwartz was kind enough to spend time talking with me about his perspective on basketball gambling and March Madness activity.

My understanding of the nuances of fandom was aided enormously by sports information directors who were willing to grant me press passes to watch games, attend postgame press conferences, and witness all that goes on behind the scenes at basketball events. Specific thanks to K. J. Cardinal, the former sports information director of the America East Conference, who was extraordinarily helpful not only in allowing me to watch games from a different vantage point but also by connecting me with other sports information directors who allowed me similar access. In addition, thanks to Kurt Svoboda at Harvard University, Jon Gust from the Big East, Jon Litchfield from the

Colonial Athletic Association, Jill Skotarczak from the Metro Athletic Association Conference, and Brian DePasquale from the University at Albany. My introduction to K. J. Cardinal was facilitated by the efforts of a former student, Tim Troville, who now is the assistant director of athletics at Indiana State University. Without Tim I would not have met K. J., and without K. J. a good portion of my understanding of fandom would have been limited. Thanks also to my colleague Peter Roby, the athletic director at Northeastern University and a former Harvard University coach and Dartmouth University player, who provided information about the NCAA tournament from the perspective of a college administrator.

To all those people who provided stories at the events I attended as members of the press corps I am forever grateful. Special thanks to Mike Zhe, the beat writer for the University of New Hampshire basketball team, and David Scott of Scott's Shots. I met Mike at a number of America East games and I sat next to David at the 2007 Colonial Athletic Association championship tournament. Both Mike and David were very informative, welcoming, and helpful to someone who did not know his way around the press table and protocol. Similarly helpful along these lines were Bruce Bosley, assistant director of athletic communications at the University of Vermont; Tony Adams, from WCAX TV3 in Burlington; Mark Brown, who has covered March Madness for ESPN's international audiences; freelance TV and sports announcer David Greenwald; and Jeffrey Rubin, president and CEO of Internet Consulting Services.

I cannot complete this acknowledgment section without thanking my regular Thursday night tennis doubles partners, Larry Donaldson, Ray Faulkner, and Carl Morris, who endured weekly reports of this project for several years. I thank you for listening to me during water breaks and for your encouragement.

I imagine that there is not much that is more difficult than living with an author with a deadline. My dear companion, Donna Glick, read many sections of this manuscript, listened to my concerns regarding this paragraph and that, and remained supportive—despite my bouts of irascibility—offering encouraging words and ideas that made me feel good and made the book stronger.

There is no way, of course, to personally thank the dozens of people I met in Las Vegas while attending the games. (When referring to people I encountered, I have not used their real names even when I knew them.) The heart of this book centers on the conversations I had with these people, who, as I hope I have made clear, have a passion that, while inexplicable to some, is nevertheless in my eyes enviable and admirable. So, to Arnie, and the Grateful Red, and Denny, and Mickey, and all others who talked with me, thank you for your involvement, however inadvertent.

Atlantic Coast Conference. A strong college basketball conference. Several teams from this conference are typically invited
to the NCAA tournament each year. The conference includes the
University of North Carolina, Duke, and Maryland.

America East. A relatively weak college basketball conference.
Only one team from this conference is likely to be invited to play
in the NCAA tournament each year. The conference includes the
University of Vermont and the University at Albany.

at large bid. An invitation to the NCAA basketball tournament
extended to a team that has not won its conference championship but is considered by the selection committee to be worthy
of participating in the tournament.

automatic bid. An invitation to the NCAA basketball tournament
extended to the champion of a conference. With the exception
of the Ivy League, conference champions are determined by an
intraleague tournament that precedes the NCAA tournament.

bid. An invitation to the NCAA basketball tournament.

Big Ten. A strong college basketball conference. Several teams from the Big Ten are typically invited to the NCAA tournament each year. The conference includes Ohio State, Indiana, Illinois, and Purdue.

bracket(s). A group of teams that play each other in a tournament; also, a diagram that represents the series of games that make up a tournament.

Colonial Athletic Association. A mid-major college basketball conference. One or two teams from this conference are typically invited to participate in the NCAA tournament each year. The conference includes Virginia Commonwealth University, George Mason University, and Northeastern.

cover. To win a game by more points than the spread, in the case of a favorite; also, to lose a game by fewer points than the spread, in the case of an underdog.

dog. *See* underdog.

favorite. The team that bookmakers expect to win a particular game.

Final Four. The semifinals and national championship game of the NCAA basketball tournament, contested by four teams, one from each region.

futures. A bet in a sports book in which the bettor wagers on what will happen in a season or a tournament in the future.

gimmee. *See* lock.

lay. To bet on a favorite with a spread of a given number of points. *See also* lumber.

line. During March Madness, the point spread. Not to be confused with the money line.

lock. A wager that a bettor believes is certain to be won.

lumber. The size of the spread; typically used to refer to a large spread. To "lay the lumber" is to bet on a large spread, that is, to advance the underdog many points.

March Madness. The NCAA men's basketball tournament, a three-week annual event that begins in March and ends in early April.

mid-major. A college basketball conference that is not as strong as a major conference such as the ACC or Big Ten, but is stronger than a minor conference such as the Colonial Athletic Association or the Missouri Valley Conference.

money line. A bet made on a team to win, regardless of the spread.

over. *See* over-under.

over-under. The predicted total number of points that both teams in a contest will score.

PAC 12. A strong college basketball conference. Several teams from the PAC 12 are typically invited to the NCAA tournament each year. The conference includes UCLA, USC, Arizona, and Washington.

parlay. A bet in which the bettor is successful only if a combination of several teams win or cover.

point spread. *See* spread.

proposition bets. Bets offered by a casino on incidental or peripheral aspects of a game, such as whether a given player will make more 3-point baskets than another player will make foul shots, or whether a given team will score more points than a golfer's score in a tournament played on the same day.

push. A bet that results in a tie between the bettor and the casino.

Regionals. The third and fourth rounds of the NCAA basketball tournament from which winners of each of the four regions emerge to play in the Final Four.

SEC. A strong college conference. Several teams from this conference are typically invited to the NCAA tournament each year. The conference includes Kentucky, Arkansas, Florida, and Vanderbilt.

seed. Ranking of a team in the NCAA basketball tournament relative to the records or perceived strength of other teams. In each region, the strongest team is the 1 seed and the weakest team is the 16 seed.

sports book. The place in a casino where bettors place wagers on sporting events.

spread. A bookmaker's assessment of the difference, in terms of points, between the stronger and weaker teams in a game.

spread bets. A bet made on the spread, as opposed to a bet made on the money line.

teasers. Cards found in sports books that list odds and parlay payouts.

under. *See* over-under.

underdog. The team that bookmakers expect to lose a given game.

vig, vigorish. The commission a casino takes on a winning bet, usually $1 on a $10 bet; for example, winning payout on a $10 bet is usually $19.